Your
Neighborhood
Gives Me the
Creeps

About the Author

Adam Selzer is the author of several books for young readers, including the forthcoming *Smart Aleck's Guide to American History* and I *Kissed a Zombie and* I *Liked It.* Because writing only keeps him occupied until about 10 a.m. most days, he has spent much of his time working as a professional ghost investigator since 2005. He is the chief historian for the Weird Chicago company and sits on the board of the American Ghost Society, in addition to running ghost tours and historical tours both for Weird Chicago and privately for student groups. He lives in Chicago (of course) with his wife and plays in a rock band called The Broken Chimneys. Check him out online at www. adamselzer.com.

True Tales of an Accidental Ghost Hunter

Your Neighborhood Gives Me the Creeps

Adam Selzer

Llewellyn Publications
Woodbury, Minnesota

First Edition
First Printing, 2009

Chapter art by Llewellyn Art Department
Cover art © iStockphoto
Cover design by Kevin R. Brown
Photograph on page 264 © Ronica Selzer, all other photographs © Adam Selzer

Llewellyn is a registered trademark of Llewellyn Worldwide, Ltd.

Library of Congress Cataloging-in-Publication Data
Selzer, Adam.
  Your neighborhood gives me the creeps : true tales of an accidental ghost hunter /
Adam Selzer.—1st ed.
    p. cm.
  ISBN 978-0-7387-1557-5
  1. Ghosts—Research—Methodology. 2. Parapsychology—Investigation. I. Title.
BF1461.S39 2009
133.1—dc22

                                                                    2009019298

Llewellyn Worldwide does not participate in, endorse, or have any authority or responsibility concerning private business transactions between our authors and the public.
  All mail addressed to the author is forwarded but the publisher cannot, unless specifically instructed by the author, give out an address or phone number.
  Any Internet references contained in this work are current at publication time, but the publisher cannot guarantee that a specific location will continue to be maintained. Please refer to the publisher's website for links to authors' websites and other sources.

Llewellyn Publications
A Division of Llewellyn Worldwide, Ltd.
2143 Wooddale Drive, Dept. 978-0-7387-1557-5
Woodbury, Minnesota 55125-2989, U.S.A.
www.llewellyn.com

Printed in the United States of America

"You don't believe in me," observed the Ghost.

"I don't," said Scrooge.

"What evidence would you have of my reality, beyond that of your senses?"

"I don't know," said Scrooge.

"Why do you doubt your senses?"

"Because," said Scrooge, "a little thing affects them. A slight disorder of the stomach makes them cheats. You may be an undigested bit of beef, a blot of mustard, a crumb of cheese, a fragment of an underdone potato. There's more of gravy than of grave about you, whatever you are!"

—Charles Dickens, A *Christmas Carol*

Contents

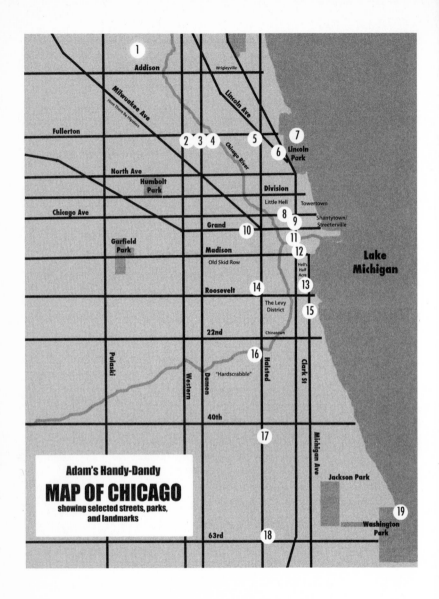

Map Key

1. Old Town Tatu (formerly Odin Tatu)
2. Our Lady of the Underpass (the Virgin Mary Salt Stain)
3. H. H. Holmes's "glass-bending factory"
4. The Liar's Club (a haunted bar; frequent tour stop)
5. Biograph Theatre/"Dillinger's Alley"
6. St. Valentine's Day Massacre site
7. Old City Cemetery/the Couch Tomb (the last remaining crypt in City Cemetery)
8. Weird Chicago Tours starting point
9. Old courthouse/jail/gallows site (fewer ghosts than you'd think!)
10. Adam's neighborhood
11. *Eastland* disaster site
12. Iroquois Theater/Death Alley
13. Congress Hotel
14. Hull House
15. Lincoln funeral train stopping point
16. Home of Bad, Bad Leroy Brown
17. Union Stockyards
18. H. H. Holmes's "murder castle" site
19. 1893 World's Fair site

Prologue

One of the more popular stories on the ghost tours I run in Chicago is "The Legend of Dillinger's Ding-a-ling." It's not a ghost story exactly, but it's too good a story not to tell.

When we run the tour on routes that go past the alley in which John Dillinger, the Depression-era bank robber, was shot, I usually tell people the popular urban legend that Dillinger's twenty-three-inch penis is on display somewhere in the Smithsonian Institute. Then I show off the picture that started the legend—a newspaper shot of Dillinger's corpse on public display at the morgue, covered from the neck down by a sheet. Rigor mortis had caused his right arm to be bent at a ninety-degree angle, resulting in a large, tentlike protrusion in the sheet just about level with Dillinger's crotch. It does look for all the world like

Dillinger's corpse is phenomenally well endowed and awfully happy to be there on the slab. Most of the onlookers surrounding the stiff (pun intended) in the picture look pretty impressed, except for one woman who looks distinctly unamused.

It is, in fact, just his arm causing the protrusion, not his wiener. No chunk of Dillinger is actually on display in the Smithsonian. One nurse—presumably the unamused woman in the picture—who tended to the corpse claimed that she peeked under the sheet out of curiosity and found that there was nothing remarkable about ol' Johnny in the crotch department. But the rumors inspired by the picture persist to this day, and the picture is usually a big hit.

However, every now and then, there'll be a crowd for whom that story isn't particularly appropriate—a crowd with a lot of young kids, for instance, or a crowd of insecure guys who might get jealous. Or sometimes the traffic keeps us from moving at normal speed, so the story is done before we even get to Diversey Avenue. Whichever is the case, it creates a few minutes of quiet time as the bus travels between Dillinger's Alley and the old factory where Adolph Luetgert, the original sausage king of Chicago, murdered his wife. I have to kill time somehow.

"Well," I ask, "are there any questions? Even if it's a totally off-the-wall question. This is *Weird* Chicago Tours, after all."

One person raises her hand, and I point at her with a flashlight. I already have a pretty good idea what's coming.

"So, do you really believe in ghosts, or what?" she asks.

I take a deep breath.

That's a loaded question.

What, exactly, is a ghost, anyway? If I say I believe in them, are the people on the bus going to think I believe every story I hear about ghostly kids pushing cars over railroad tracks, every story about guys in white sheets who rattle chains and go "Whoooo"? Will they think I believe that a translucent version of me is floating around in my body, ready to fly free when I die?

I spend a lot of energy trying to keep from seeming like a total nut, and saying I believe in ghosts—any kind of ghosts—will make me look like a nut to many people right away.

When we say "ghost," we usually think of the Hollywood model: a translucent version of a dead person that floats around wearing ghostly clothes that, while translucent themselves, still manage to cover up the ghost's hoohoos perfectly. According to the stories attached to ghosts, this is usually supposed to be the soul of the dead person; either the soul is unable to "move on" or it's back from some celestial plane to sort out unfinished business. Do I have to believe in that stuff to believe in ghosts?

And what about the similar apparitions that we call "residual" hauntings—these look like Hollywood ghosts, but they aren't thought to be conscious entities. They're sort of like video recordings that play over and over again, no more aware of themselves than, say, the wind or the waves in Lake Michigan. Some theorize that these residual hauntings are caused by some sort of energy exerted at the moment of sudden, traumatic deaths, creating a sort of "mental picture." If that's true, do these count as ghosts, too, or do ghosts have to be intelligent, thinking beings to qualify?

In fact, those are just two of the countless kinds of ghosts that people talk about. You need a whole encyclopedia to cover all of them.

There are poltergeists—ghosts that can't be seen, but manifest by turning lights off and on, throwing things around the room, tugging at your clothes, and generally making nuisances of themselves.

There are figures so lifelike that you can dance with them all night and never realize that they're not regular, living people until they disappear out of your car as you drive them past the suburban cemetery on South Archer Avenue.

There are vague voices heard in empty houses and hallways. Sometimes they seem intelligent enough to communicate; sometimes they just seem to repeat the same word or phrase over and over again.

There are mysterious phantom houses that appear near a cemetery, disappear, then show up again on the other side of the graveyard.

Spooky faces that just appear for a split second in the mirror. Spookier faces that jump *out* of the mirror and try to bite you.

Strange forces that cause people to get hang-up phone calls from a number once owned by a long-dead friend or cause a grandfather clock to stop with its hands frozen at 3:10, the time when the clock's owner passed away.

Residual emotional energies that leave "bad vibes" in a place where a murder or disaster took place. Some say that these same energies cause the feelings of fright that come to people in darkened rooms with creaking doors and creeping shadows.

Which of these count as ghosts? Are any of them "real" to begin with, or are all of them just figments of overactive imaginations? If it's the latter, is there any value in telling stories about them at all or in researching them scientifically? Am I just wasting everyone's time or, worse, encouraging people to jump to supernatural explanations for everyday occurrences by taking them on ghost hunts?

Without question, most of the ghost reports I hear can be explained away with the knowledge you'll find in any eighth-grade science book. Any ghost hunter worth his salt will tell you that at least 80 percent of all ghost reports can be dismissed very quickly.

But others are a bit harder to account for. Science may eventually find a way that a traumatic, sudden death can produce some form of energy that will, under certain unusual conditions, manifest as an "apparition." Anything's possible.

Some scientists say that for ghosts to exist, we'd have to rearrange physics, but for some ghosts, we may just have to learn more *about* physics.

Or perhaps we don't need to rearrange physics at all; we just need to rearrange semantics. Whether ghosts are real or not depends a lot on what counts as a ghost and what doesn't. One thing I can say for sure is that there are weird things in the environment that can have the psychological effect of making you *think* there's a dead person hanging around. Should the wind making a moaning noise by blowing over a hole in the roof count as a ghost? It certainly functions as a ghost for all practical purposes, after all.

I'm a skeptic. Or, anyway, I try to be. I think that just about everything (except for Bob Dylan) can be explained by science. Even the stuff that we can't explain *yet* will probably be explained eventually. And it's a good thing I'm a skeptic; I've had my palm read twice, and both readers told me I'd die in a bus accident. On the tours, I stand up at the front of a bus for long stretches of time—with the door open in summer.

But there are only a few blocks of space between the end of the "appropriate for all audiences" version of the John Dillinger story and the sausage factory. I don't have time to explain all of this. I just have time to break out a quick stock response.

"Well," I say, "I don't believe everything I hear, but I *have* seen some pretty weird stuff."

I have, in fact, seen some strange things. I've seen shadows cast next to my own on the wall when there was no one next to me. I've heard weird voices and ghostly music. I've heard gunshots ringing out in empty hallways. I've felt invisible hands tapping me on the shoulder and flicking my ear.

In fact, I've experienced almost all of those things at one particular location.

And it just happens to be the next stop on the tour.

"If I Die in This Place..."

**ODIN TATU, 3313 W. Irving Park,
Chicago, IL, June, 2006.**

When people become ghosts, they're generally expected to haunt the places where they died. According to most of the scientific (well, pseudoscientific) theories that seek to explain ghosts, what we know as a ghost is probably caused by a jolt of some sort of mental energy, usually at the moment of a sudden, traumatic death, and this left-over energy will only be strong enough to manifest in a way that we'd be able to notice it at the place it was first exerted.

However, by this logic, how do we explain the number of haunted cemeteries that are reported? Practically nobody dies in the cemetery, and, when they do, it can't be all that traumatic—in fact, it's sort of convenient, in a way. The same goes for funeral parlors; they might have had a few stiffs on the embalming table who weren't quite dead yet, but, hey, you're already on the slab, right? Might as well get embalmed while you're there. Dying of being embalmed when you're already in a coma probably won't bring forth the same jolt of mental energy that dying of falling six stories into an alley when you're already on fire would.

But we do hear a lot about haunted cemeteries and funeral parlors. Some people think that the sheer outpouring of emotion that goes on in these places leaves a sort of impact on the environment that can "create" a ghost. Ghostly funerals aren't unheard of. For instance, many people who lived near spots where Abraham Lincoln's funeral train rolled through in the 1860s reported "ghost trains" appearing occasionally for more than a century after Lincoln had been buried. And some people think that there may be some mysterious earthly energies that led early settlers to put a graveyard or undertaking parlor in a given location in the first place.

When I hear about haunted cemeteries, I don't usually jump right into speculating that there's some sort of emotional residue or mysterious energy in the air. I usually just assume that teenagers probably snuck in to get high and started seeing things that they thought were ghosts. And I'm almost always right. In fact, let's call this Selzer's First Theorem: *Any remotely spooky place that people sneak into in order to get wasted will eventually turn up on a TV show, website, or book about ghosts.*

So, when Ken Melvoin-Berg, one of my partners in the ghost tour business, called me and told me we were going to investigate a haunted tattoo parlor called Odin Tatu, which used to be a funeral home, I figured it was probably just some place where the owners were seeing weird things in a drug-induced haze and blaming it on dead guys. It happens all the time.

Hence, my first question to Ken was "What are they on?"

"Oh, probably plenty," said Ken. "The owner is a guy named Tapeworm. I don't think he realizes that he knows me, though. I used to be a bouncer and roving psychic at a club where he hung out about five years ago."

I added this to my master list of Weird Jobs Ken Has Had, which, by now, also included Maroon Beret, EMT, soup chef, game designer, incense salesman, and porn star. And psychic detective, of course. That was his regular day job.

At the time, Ken, an author named Troy Taylor, and I were running Olga Durlochen's Chicago Spooks ghost tour company. Troy had taken over the business end of the company about a year or so before when Olga's husband went to jail for arson. He handled reservations, marketing, and stuff like that, while Ken and I took turns running the tours aboard a bus.

On the side, we also conducted investigations of sup-posedly haunted places around the city. We weren't one of the more formal ghost-hunting groups around; we didn't have uniforms or a team name or company song or mis-sion statement or anything like that, like many groups do. Honestly, we thought that those were sort of corny. Part of the reason I got into the ghostbusting business was so that I could *quit* working for companies that had lame mission statements. If someone really pressed us for a name, we'd say we were called Captain Spooky McGuffin and his Para-normal Posse. We took turns being Captain Spooky.

Troy Taylor's name was particularly well known in the ghost business. He had, at the time, written over thirty books on history and hauntings. His books generally fo-cused more on the history behind the ghost stories than the "evidence," so I could read them as a skeptic and not think he was a maniac.

Ken Melvoin-Berg, who had brought me into the com-pany some time before, had a reputation of his own. His grandfather was a psychic of some repute, and he himself had been trained by Irene Hughes, who had made a name for herself by predicting the Kennedy assassinations. Al-most needless to say, Ken is a little less skeptical about ghosts and other strange phenomena than I am.

As a skeptic, I'm naturally quite suspicious of psychics. I get customers on the tours who claim to be psychic all the time. Usually, it's fairly obvious that they're really just nuts. Sometimes they'll tell me there are fairies on my shoulder or a gremlin on the side of the bus. Others are clearly just using the same tricks phony psychics have been using for decades upon decades. Ken, however, has impressed me on enough occasions for me to at least give him the benefit of the doubt. If he tells me that the best place to investigate in a haunted house is some particular room or another, I have no reason not to give that room a shot.

Still, even with his assurance that the place was pretty spooky, I was quite leery of investigating the tattoo parlor, since it seemed like just another somewhat spooky place where people get wasted and think they're seeing stuff. But our investigations were almost always great fun. If nothing else, a ghost investigation is a great excuse to go poking around old buildings looking for cool stuff like secret passages, hidden chambers, and nifty antique furnishings. And Ken assured me that Odin still had plenty of architectural details from the days when it was the Klemundt Funeral Home, which the building had served as for several decades.

The records we have on the place contradict each other, which is not uncommon in Chicago, where hardly a building went up in the late nineteenth and early twentieth centuries without some worker or another needing to cover his tracks. But it appears that the Klemundt Funeral Home building was built around 1923 and that it was built over the foundation of an earlier undertaking parlor that is said to have been built in the 1880s. The original foundation is still present, functioning as the spooky basement that no haunted house is complete without.

There was plenty left in the tattoo parlor to remind visitors of the building's history, like stained-glass windows, woodwork said to have been salvaged from a ruined South Side mansion, and a gorgeous mosaic fireplace in the entryway. Rumor has it that the gate on the front door had been the doorway to the German village in the 1933 World's Fair. Rumor also has it that there had once been a graveyard out back, near the former stable (which is now a garage), serving as a resting place for somewhere over thirty bodies. Given the fact that the building was an undertaking establishment, this is quite likely to be true. And given the fact that it's Chicago, it's also quite likely that the bodies are still there. Chicago has a real habit of moving tombstones and leaving the bodies buried beneath them behind.

On the day of the investigation, Ken and I began with a quick survey around the premises. The first thing that struck me as interesting was the fireplace in the entryway—the mosaic work on it was done by the Tiffany company, we were told. Inside the fireplace, where one would normally put firewood, there was a gravestone dated 1957.

"We found that in the attic," said Nick, a tattoo artist. "But it made us all nervous having it be up there, so we brought it down where we could keep an eye on it. It took, like, five of us to move the thing."

It was an elegant building, full of ancient stonework, wooden archways, and all of the other classy touches that one expects in an old funeral parlor. But, for contrast, it also had tattoo facilities, loud music, spooky masks on the wall, a lot of things that looked voodoo-related, and a whole bunch of cool Star Wars stuff, including a life-sized statue of Yoda wearing a fedora, which is the kind of thing that you don't see in nearly enough funeral parlors. I'll just say right here that when I die, there had *better* be a life-sized Yoda at the funeral. I'm flexible on the fedora—a bowler cap will do—but I'm adamant about the Yoda.

Gradually, the rest of the crew for the evening showed up. Hector, an improv comic who usually drove the bus for me on the tours I ran, was there. Also joining us were two teenage girls that I hadn't met before.

"This is Kaytlyn and Keegan," Ken said, indicating the girls. "They're both very good natural psychics. I've known them since they were babies. Both of them are clairaudient, which means they hear things, and Keegan is clairsentient, like me, which means she feels things. And they tend to have stronger powers when they're around each other."

Kaytlyn couldn't stay on the investigation long, since she was leaving for China the next morning, where she'd be attending a cheerleading camp. For a second there, I sort of felt like one of those sitcom characters who finds out that the doctor performing his coronary bypass is a twelve-year-old prodigy. I'm skeptical of psychics to begin with, and I'd had perhaps a dozen teenagers on the tour who had convinced themselves that they were psychic. Most of them were real pains in the ass.

But at least they weren't old enough to be senile, like most of the supposed psychics I met. And, as Hector pointed out to me, Ken could be rather arrogant about his psychic abilities and tended not to believe that anyone *else* was psychic. His seal of approval on Keegan and Kaytlyn was a pretty big deal.

"Isn't Olga coming?" I asked Ken.

"She'll be along later, I hope," said Ken. "I haven't heard from her, though. And Ray's back in town."

We were all a bit nervous about Ray, Olga's husband, who had been let out of prison a few days before. Ray was, shall we say, a gentleman of somewhat uncertain character.

About a year or so before, Ray had had a bit of an episode. According to newspaper reports, he had stabbed Olga's mattress with a knife, left a note saying she was next, and left a message on an answering machine belonging to her brother, a police sergeant, threatening to do all sorts of colorful things to him with a screwdriver. He then set fire to a portion of the church where the tour bus was parked when not in use. One can imagine how we'd be a bit wary about the guy. Olga herself had said at his trial that he'd "keep doing this forever."

Ken and I were about halfway sure that Olga and Ray were going to restart the company from scratch, putting Ray in charge and doing all the tours themselves, and putting us out of our jobs. I was a lot more nervous about this than I was about running into a ghost that night. But we had to keep this out of our minds for the moment—we had an investigation to do.

When everyone, except for Olga, had arrived, we were introduced to Tapeworm, the owner. He had come into possession of the parlor a few years before, naming it after his son, Odin.

"You're Santeria, aren't you?" said Hector when they were introduced.

"Yeah," said Tapeworm, with a knowing nod. "You too."

Santeria is an Afro-Caribbean religion not unlike voodoo in many ways, except that, unlike voodoo, it actually *does* involve some animal sacrifice. Neither Hector nor Tapeworm actually practiced it; but both Hector and Tapeworm were of Cuban descent—Tapeworm was born in Havana—and had been raised around aunts and grandmothers who spoke about it frequently. And they spotted it in each other right away. Hector claimed that people from the Santeria tradition could always spot each other.

Of course, Ken claimed that Hector didn't know anything about Santeria. "He's not even Cuban, he's Puerto Rican," Ken said when I asked him about it later. Ken and Hector picked on each other to no end—they were like brothers. But, like brothers, they were fiercely protective of each other. If anyone *else* picked on Hector, Ken got mad.

Hector may have guessed that Tapeworm had some connection to Santeria because he recognized some of the masks and symbols that were set up around the parlor—Tapeworm was especially fond of Chango, a Santeria orisha (spirit) known as the god of thunder and lightning. I knew nothing about Santeria, except that it was known to involve animal sacrifice and that, according to Ken, there was a temple for it in the backyard of an apartment about four blocks from mine. I was never sure if Ken was serious, but if there was anybody in Chicago who knew where to go to see a chicken sacrificed, it was Ken.

As usual, after scoping the place out, we started out the investigation by interviewing the people who worked in the building, starting with a new guy who told us that he'd recently heard something going "Whoooo" in the basement, where they used to do all of the embalming. As soon as he said this, Hector and I looked at each other, trying not to laugh.

One of the jokes we liked to play between stops on our tours was having customers play "scare the tourist" by making ghost noises out the windows of the bus at the passers-by on Michigan Avenue. Invariably, they would all go "Whooooooooo," and the passers-by would look on, halfway between amused and annoyed (except for one Amish couple, who were just plain annoyed). I would then point out to the people that I had never, ever heard of an actual ghost that made a noise like that. You hear of moaning noises now and then, but "Whoooo" is the kind of noise ghosts only make in cartoons.

I'm pretty sure that all ghost hunters, believers and skeptics alike, will agree with me when I say that, if a witness says the ghost went "Whoooo," it means one of three things:

1. The witness is lying (or stoned) (or both).

2. It is, in fact, just the wind blowing through a hole in the wall or something, creating an effect not unlike the one you get by blowing over the rim of a pop bottle or moonshine jug.

3. It's not a ghost at all—it's Old Man Peters, the man who ran the haunted amusement park! And he would have gotten away with it, too, if it weren't for those meddling kids!

So this guy was not only quite likely lying, he wasn't even doing a very good job of it.

Most of the rest of the staff, however, told more plausible stories. Some of them told stories about poltergeist-style activity—shelves falling apart inside of glass display cases, ashtrays flying across the room and landing upside without spilling a single ash. One of the scarier masks—a Japanese one that Keegan found especially frightening—had a tendency to fall off of the wall and onto the floor.

A couple of people had more interesting stories than this. Some told of seeing, hearing, or "feeling" the ghost of a little blonde girl in the front entryway, near the fireplace, and the stairway that led to the apartment upstairs. But Tapeworm, perhaps a bit predictably, had the most interesting stories.

He told us about seeing a woman in a white gown walking up to the counter and a guy in a powder-blue suit that he'd seen walking across an archway near the main studio—apparently the ghosts of some poor sap who died in the 1970s.

"There's also this guy I've seen twice who wears a brown suit," he said. "Looks like he's in his sixties or seventies, and he's dressed, I don't know, like it's the nineteen twenties or thirties. I saw him a couple of weeks ago, standing there, like he was looking at me while I was over here tattooing. And I stopped what I was doing and tried to motion for other people to look, but I wouldn't take my eye off him for one second, man, cause I knew that if I looked away for a second, he'd be gone. And he was! The second I looked away, he vanished."

I was reasonably sure, at the time, that Tapeworm's stories were either lies or based on hallucinations—the woman in white, in particular, was a bit of a giveaway. When people tell me about a ghostly woman in white (which they frequently do), it's a pretty safe bet that they're just telling me what they think I want to hear.

I once spoke to a police officer who told me that when people tell police that they were attacked by a "stranger with bushy hair," the police assume that they're lying. Similarly, people who are making up a ghost story almost always seem to go with either a woman in a long white gown or a little kid playing with a ball. Of course, this doesn't mean I can brush off the stories automatically; just as the police know that there must be a handful of bushy-haired strangers out there committing crimes, I have no way to know that there isn't some celestial bureaucracy that issues white dresses to dead women and rubber balls to dead children. Maybe it's the same place that gave Jacob Marley his chains.

And it was impossible not to like Tapeworm. His enthusiasm for his work and the building were infectious, and he was a much better storyteller than anyone else we met that day. He was, at the very least, quite a character. One of my favorite things about the job was meeting people like him. You really do meet the weirdos when you work in the ghost business.

Tapeworm might, in fact, have had a checkered past, but he was now apparently living clean and was a respected member of the neighborhood. Neighbors who had been apprehensive about having a tattoo parlor in their midst (as opposed to the incessant cheeriness of a funeral home) were won over by his personality, as was everyone on the investigation. No one who actually knew him personally, rather than by reputation, seemed to have a bad thing to say about him.

Ken, Hector, and I all decided right away that most of the people in the building weren't making up the ghosts, exactly—they'd probably seen a few things that they couldn't explain, but some of the things they were telling us were likely just the result of their imaginations taking over after they heard that the place was haunted. Only one story has to be true to make a place haunted for real, though.

"Now, here's what really freaks me out," Tapeworm said, continuing to regale us with ghost stories. "Check out those stairs over there."

He pointed over to the main staircase. The old, art deco–tiled stairs led up to a stained-glass window where the staircase curved around.

"I remember being a kid in this neighborhood, and you could see those stairs in the window. I was always all superstitious about it, because of what the place was, you know. It was where the dead people were."

I sympathized. A natural outgrowth of my childhood fear of cemeteries had been a general fear of funeral homes. I hated going with my family to pick up my brother at Little League practice, because his team practiced near a funeral home, which meant there was a chance that I might see an actual coffin. I still don't know how they managed to get any baseball practice in with that place looming behind them.

"So I tried to avoid looking at it," Tapeworm continued. "And now, you know, things change around, and lo and behold, thirty years later, I'm *living* here. And twice, when I've been walking down those stairs, I felt like something was trying to push me!"

"Like, push you down the stairs?" I asked.

"Yeah!" he said. "And that fuckin' freaks me out, because everyone knows you can't fight *back* with these cats! So, the first time it happened, I just looked up and shouted, 'Listen, motherfucker! If I fuckin' die in this fuckin' place, it is fuckin' *on*!'"

Naturally, those stairs were the first place we wanted to investigate. And even though I had my doubts about Tapeworm's stories, the place turned out to be as spooky as all get-out that night. In fact, it was probably the spookiest place I'd ever investigated.

My job on investigations, besides doing historical research and attempting to explain away anything weird that happened, was to be in charge of electronic voice phenomenon (EVP), which meant walking around with audio gear to see if we pick up any strange sounds that might be audible on recordings, but not to the naked ear. On television, the EVP guys are usually the ones who wander around waving microphones in the air and saying, "Are there any spirits here who have a message for us?"

For the record, I don't normally do that—I'd feel like a real dork going around talking like that—but every now and then I'll say something out loud just to see if there's a response. That way, I can just analyze the audio for a couple of seconds after the question instead of listening to the whole thing for strange voices, which can be a pretty dull process.

I had recently modified my gear a bit to speed things up—I had set it up so the microphone was farther away from the recording unit, so that it wouldn't pick up any noise from the unit itself, and had set it up with a pair of signal-boosting earphones that allowed me to hear what I was recording in real time. Using a sensitive microphone, it wasn't unlike wearing a set of high-powered hearing aids. This allowed me to make a note of any unusual sounds as they happened, rather than trying to find them later.

The recorder began to act up on the staircase—it might have just been related to the air vents or the nearby neon sign, but there was an abnormal humming noise that would almost overwhelm me whenever we started going up the stairs—much more noise than I'd normally expect from a neon sign. There was something odd about that staircase, all right.

Upstairs was the main living area, where Tapeworm actually lived. It was a bit of a mess, decorated with even more life-sized Star Wars statues. But there was an undeniable spookiness about the place—some sort of "weight" in the air, like a humidity, which I attributed primarily to the fact that it was summer in Chicago and the building didn't have any air conditioning.

But some places just have a "haunted" vibe about them—something you can't define, but you can sure as hell feel. And everyone present noticed it in Tapeworm's apartment that night right away. As far as I'm concerned, these places that have that vibe count as haunted, even if the real cause is just humidity, wiring, low-frequency noise, or any of the other explanations we skeptics come up with. Once you've got a good story and that haunted vibe, all that remains is to gather some cool "evidence" and a good backstory, and you've got yourself a building that functions as haunted for all practical purposes.

That vibe, the "haunted" feeling, comes and goes at any given location. Even the most famously and reliably haunted places don't have the feeling about them all the time. On the tours, I got to where I could tell the minute we stepped off the bus whether a location was going to be "active" that night or not. Ken described this as a form of psychic ability, but I just thought of it as something similar to being able to step outside and tell whether it was raining or not.

Of course, the question to ask ourselves here is whether this feeling comes from ghosts, or if it's caused by regular ol' environmental effects (humidity, barometric pressure, etc.) that just make you *think* the place is haunted. But, for all we really know, maybe those environmental effects are what allow ghosts to manifest in the first place. You never can tell with this stuff.

Whatever the cause of that haunted vibe, I was feeling it in that upstairs living area. If picking it up was like being able to tell when it was raining, it was pouring in there.

Keegan and Kaytlyn immediately gravitated toward one particular door, which was shut.

"Can we open places?" Keegan asked.

"I don't think we should," said Ken, as we walked around the room.

But Tapeworm stepped in and told us it was fine to go in, so we did. The room behind the door was mostly empty, except for a drum set and some electrical gear. The light wouldn't come on when we hit the switch.

"Have you had any experiences in this room?" asked Ken.

"That was the first room I moved into," said Tapeworm. "I moved out within a week. Nobody can ever get a good night's sleep in here."

It wasn't difficult to see why—once again, it just had that vibe. It felt like there was something else in the room. There may be scientific explanations for this, but telling yourself it's just humidity or a low-frequency noise having a psychological effect on you frankly doesn't make a place seem any less spooky in the heat of the moment.

Ken told Keegan and Kaytlyn to walk around the room and ask the ghost some questions. This is generally not the most effective method in the world to get a ghost to show up, but it also doesn't really hurt anything, and it can help get people focused on what they're doing.

Keegan, however, wouldn't enter the room. She felt as though she simply couldn't. The rest of us soldiered on, with her watching from the threshold.

"Can we help you with anything?" Ken asked out loud. All reservations about asking questions aside, when we do get the idea that a ghost might be in the room, we usually ask if we can be helpful in any way. It's just sort of common courtesy.

"It doesn't need help," said Kaytlyn, confidently.

Hector fumbled with the light switch, but it wasn't working. "This was an office at one time," said Ken, using his superpowers.

Meanwhile, in my earphone, I was hearing the faint sound of slow organ music—not unlike a funeral dirge—coming from somewhere in the room. It would be audible, if faint, on the recording later—mostly single whole notes, but at least one three-note chord could be heard, indicating that it wasn't just a vibration in the room. I didn't pick it up in any other places in the building.

"There's a temperature drop in here, too," Hector whispered. "And it smells different."

Keegan and Kaytlyn both seemed fairly exasperated by the room—even though Keegan hadn't set foot inside—and I was, too. It was an intense experience just standing in that room. I knew, of course, that if we came back the next night, it might feel fine in there. We were lucky—we happened to be investigating on an active night. One problem I have with ghost-hunting TV shows is that the investigators on the shows are usually only in a location for a few nights (and it's usually edited down to make it look like only one). Whether the place is active while they're there or not is sort of luck of the draw; places can be active for months, then inactive for years.

Meanwhile, over in the kitchen, a couple of Tapeworm's friends chatted, smoked, and listened to music. If they were setting us up to fake us out, they were doing a terrible job of it. People trying to fake us wouldn't be so careless as to have extra people just hanging around the house; they probably would have planned the night out in great detail and not left anything to chance. I wasn't convinced that all of Tapeworm's stories were true, but I was reasonably sure that they weren't trying to trick us.

Ken directed us out, back into the living room area.

"Cool bed," said Hector, noticing Tapeworm's bed, which featured enormous angel wings above the headboard.

Tapeworm told us that he'd made the bed himself and that he had poured all the suffering that came out of his divorce into the bed—his "wings of freedom." He also said that his bedroom was "calm."

"There's a very different feeling in this room, for sure," said Ken.

"This is the only room where I've been able to get any sleep in the house," said Tapeworm. "But every time I have sex in here, I *know* there's something watching me!"

We all had a good laugh—a lot of investigations have a "no smoking and no joking" rule, but it's very useful to joke around now and then if you've just been spooked out, even if it was just a spooky, empty room. The Captain Spooky team tended to break the no-joking rule a *lot*.

"The window opens by itself all the time," said Tape-worm. "And the bathroom window, too, right while I'm sitting there. And I'll go, 'Gee, it smells that bad, huh?'"

Just as I was admiring a life-sized Darth Maul statue near the bedroom, the sound of Star Wars music came from Ken's cell phone.

"That's gotta be Olga," said Hector.

"It's Troy," said Ken. "Not Olga. Hang on."

Ken ran out to a balcony to take the call, and I took control of the investigation for a second.

"Shit," said Hector. "He's telling him we've all been fired. I know it."

"Shit," I agreed.

Ken popped back into the room.

"Girls," he said, "I have to take this outside. Follow Adam, he's going to help you with the investigation." Ken stepped out onto the balcony, and the rest of us started to head downstairs, with me leading the way.

I decided to lead the group back down to the main floor. We all grabbed tight on to the railing of the stairs, making jokes about not wanting to get pushed down the stairs. As we did, I thought I heard some sort of laughter coming from the walls in my earphones.

"It's making fun of us," said Kaytlyn, who didn't know I was picking up the laughter. "The ghost. It thinks it's funny that we think we're going to be pushed. 'Cause it's not gonna push us."

"Well, that's pleasant, anyway," I said.

The laugh was very clear on the recording—I didn't even have to turn it up to hear it clearly. My first thought was that it was the little girl ghost, but it didn't seem like she'd have much to laugh about, and, anyway, it sounded more like an adult laugh. Actually, it sounded like the love child of Fran Drescher and Krusty the Clown. Scary.

When Ken returned, we lingered around the tattoo parlor, letting Tapeworm show us what he thought was once an embalming room. Ken talked to Hector for just a second, then began to lead us to the basement.

"Do you know what Troy wanted?" I whispered to Hector.

"Don't worry about that for now," he said. "Just focus on the investigation."

"Are we all fired?" I asked.

"No!" he said, as though I'd just said something really stupid. "We're not fired! Let's go!"

So, with great relief, I headed down the creaky back staircase into the basement, the supposed foundation of the funeral parlor from the 1880s, over which the current structure had been built. Not long before, I wouldn't have gone to the basement of such a place on a bet, but the relief of knowing I still had a job overcame any nervousness.

You can probably imagine that the basement of an old funeral parlor is going to be a reasonably frightening place. It was a musty, open space with a ceiling of exposed beams barely six feet above the floor, eroded by years of termites. There were only a few bare bulbs to light the entire area. A quick look around showed a casket-sized hole in the wall—supposedly used to pass caskets to hearses, or something like that. We found a drainage area, and the probable location of an incinerator.

While a record proving the place had been a funeral parlor in the 1880s hasn't turned up yet, the basement was clearly much older than the rest of the building. We could easily see where the windows were, back when the building was the first floor, not a basement. Many Chicago basements were the first floors of buildings before the street levels were raised to make more room for sewers decades ago. Richer people could have their buildings raised, but most people just turned the first floor into the basement. Many of these basements became apartments that Realtors cheerfully refer to as "garden level" today.

We wandered through the basement, gravitating toward the northeast corner.

"It's over here!" Kaytlyn said, confidently.

As I stepped into the corner, facing the wall, I felt someone tapping me on the shoulder, and I turned expecting to see Hector, but found nobody there.

The corner also felt remarkably cold—there was a temperature drop that seemed as though it couldn't have been less than twenty degrees. In a building without air conditioning in Chicago in June, this is off the charts.

"There's something here," I said. "Something is very strange right here." Sometimes I turn some of my skepticism off during investigations in order to just "let things happen." We can usually hold off on analyzing things until the next day.

"What's your name?" Kaytlyn called out.

Just then, through the earphone, I distinctly heard a voice. It sounded like it was coming from far away, even though we were against the wall.

"Walter!" it said.

I was stunned.

"Did it just say its name was Walter?" I asked.

"Yes, it did," said Kaytlyn, confidently.

I realized right away that I'd made a mistake. I shouldn't have said the name out loud. All Kaytlyn had to do was agree with me. It would have been better if I'd said, "Are you getting anything?" and she'd said something about hearing the name "Walter" herself.

Still, I'd picked it up on the recorder. And it was clear—not like the sound of Charlie Brown's teacher, which is what most EVP sounds like. It sounded like a regular human voice. And I didn't understand why it sounded like it was coming from someone ten or twenty feet in front of me, when the only thing in front of me was a wall.

"There's something else here," said Ken. And he began to talk to the ghost, too. "What did they do to the left side of your body?" he asked. "A knife?" he paused. "Bigger than a knife?"

Meanwhile, the recorder was picking up some distant noises that sounded, if vaguely, like a person in agony.

"Can we do anything for you?" asked Ken. This time, there was nothing in my earphones to indicate any sort of response.

Just then, the light came on. Everyone jumped.

"Sorry, guys," said Hector, who was holding the cord to the light. "That was me."

Everyone let out a relieved sort of laugh. A second later, I felt the temperature in the corner warm back up to normal, and the feeling that any ghosts might have been around simply evaporated. The "haunted vibe" can come and go in a heartbeat.

"I think we got a name," I said. "I just got something saying 'Walter.'"

"It said its name was Walter?" asked Keegan, sounding rather like she didn't believe me.

"Yeah," I said.

"That was the name of the guy," she said. She didn't seem to be saying this because she had a psychic feeling about it, either. It seemed like something she'd researched.

"The name of what guy?" I asked.

"The guy who owned the funeral parlor."

"That was his name," Tapeworm confirmed. "The guy who died. There were three generations of the family who owned the place, and Walter was the last one."

"There are actually six ghosts down here," said Ken, confidently. This was the sort of thing Ken is given to saying on investigations, and I have no way to tell if he's bullshitting me. It's not like I can say, "Come on, Ken, any idiot can see there are only four." Ken is also wrong fairly often, and he's the first one to admit it.

We hung around the corner a while longer, but whatever had been there before was gone. Ken said that whatever we had picked up was a "trickster" ghost—the sort who might act all spooky, but is really just playing around. Walter might not have been the ghost's name. It might have just been calling out to someone named Walter, or it might have been just saying *a* name, confused by the question. Most ghosts, even the ones that we classify as "intelligent," don't seem to be that bright. Ken equates it to those creatures in the dark depths of the ocean that do little with their lives other than sit around, instinctively eating any creature that gets too close. They aren't exactly smart. They just have a sort of instinctual intelligence.

Nobody felt a single thing the rest of the investigation. The vibe that had been in the house before had simply ceased to be.

After we decided to call it a night, I asked Ken what the phone call had been about.

"Olga," he said. "Apparently, she was doing some press event about ghosts at Wrigley Field, and Ray showed up drunk and calling her unprintable names."

He showed me a picture of Ray so I'd know what he looked like and instructed me to call the cops if I ever saw him, since there was some worry that he was going to try to show up and commandeer the bus on an upcoming tour. Hector and I made some fighting plans, and I tried to remember what I'd learned in karate lessons back when I was seven.

Tapeworm wanted to hear the voice saying "Walter," but we were still using the recording gear. I told him I'd get it up online shortly, and we made tentative plans to do an overnight investigation at the parlor in a month or two.

After that, we dove into historical research on the place. We got a lot of different stories about Walter—some said there was no such person. Others insisted that there *was* a Walter, but he couldn't be a ghost because he wasn't quite dead yet. We did find evidence of several people named Walter whose funerals had been held in the parlor. In the end, what the ghost in the corner might have been talking about proved to be sort of inconclusive. Maybe it was the ghost of someone who had been embalmed in the building, or someone who had lived there, or maybe it was just messing with us. There's also always the chance that the voice came from someone passing by outside, randomly shouting the name "Walter" right at the time we had asked "What's your name?"

We also heard from a few members of the family who had owned the funeral parlor. They'd thought the place was haunted for *years*, which at least made me feel a little more confident that the tattoo people hadn't made the whole thing up. *Something* was in that building making people think that there were ghosts around.

I began telling stories about the ghost of Walter on the tours, along with stories about Tapeworm, whose language

I generally cleaned up considerably when I retold his stories. His story about challenging the ghosts on the staircase to a fight in the event that he died in the place was an especially big hit.

Three weeks after the investigation, Ken called me again.

"Remember Tapeworm?" he asked.

"Sure," I said. "How could I forget Tapeworm?"

"He died yesterday," said Ken.

Tapeworm had suffered a heart attack and died in his bedroom—just a few feet from the staircase.

He was thirty-seven.

In the months that followed, lots of things would change. Ray would take over Chicago Spooks, and Ken, Troy, and I would buy a bus of our own and found Weird Chicago Tours, our own outfit, in the name of job security. Hector would become Chicago Spooks's main tour guide before being fired when Ray, as we'd predicted, started doing everything himself. After that, Hector drifted out of the ghost business altogether for a while.

But Odin Tatu would just get weirder and weirder.

Who Do I Think I Am?

I'm about the least New Agey person I know. I'm no one's idea of a scientist, but I know enough to call "bullshit" on some of the more outrageous claims that I hear (and I hear a lot of them).

I don't claim to have any knowledge of "the spirit world" or any means of communicating with dead people that would elicit a response. I suppose I can't claim that I don't believe in the supernatural at all—I turn my hat inside out when the Cubs need a rally—but generally speaking, I consider myself to be a rationally minded, critical-thinking skeptic.

I wasn't always a skeptic, though. When I was ten, I was entirely convinced that there was a plesiosaur swimming around in Loch Ness, that Bigfoot made tracks all over the Northwest, and that aliens flew in from time to time to stick flashlights up hillbillies' butts. I read book after book showing murky Nessie pictures. I pored over endless analyses of the Patterson-Gimlin Bigfoot film footage and debates about the supposed UFO crash at Roswell.

I had a very low opinion of skeptics at the time, for a variety of reasons. One of the main reasons was that the TV shows and books about strange phenomenon, I now realize, tended to treat skeptics rather unfairly. The TV shows, for instance, would show photographs and evidence and interviews with wide-eyed believers and experts—and I now realize that these shows throw the term "expert" around about as freely as Disney uses the word "classic"—who assured the viewer that this stuff was for real. Then the narrator would say, "Still, some skeptics disagree," saying "skeptics" in the same tone of voice that narrators of political commercials use for the word "liberal."

Then they'd show the token skeptic, who almost invariably looked like a total wiener and always seemed bent on ruining everyone else's fun, saying that the UFO or ghost the people had seen was really just swamp gas or something equally asinine. It seemed like they were always blaming things on swamp gas—even out in the desert. Good-natured, rational skeptics didn't get a lot of airtime on those shows.

At the end, someone would say something like, "So, is it fact or fiction? You decide!" It would have been made clear by then that only a moron would go for "fiction." The whole thing strikes me as awfully silly today—you see more variations of the "you decide" line than ever nowadays, but it's not like viewers actually *get* to decide these things. What viewers decide after watching a TV show has no bearing on whether or not Bigfoot is actually real.

I read a lot of ghost stories in those days, too, but I usually insisted that I didn't believe in ghosts. It wasn't because I was actually examining the evidence critically, though—I simply didn't *want* ghosts to exist. Living in Urbandale, Iowa, a suburb of Des Moines, I was pretty safe from Scottish lake monsters, but ghosts could show up anywhere. Not believing in them was simply a mechanism to make me feel safer. It's not an uncommon trick; on the tours, the most vocally skeptical customers are almost invariably also the most frightened.

It wasn't only because I didn't want to see a ghost that I didn't want to believe in them—I also didn't want to *be* one. The idea of spending eternity floating around in someone's attic scared me out of my wits. What if I had to spend eternity walking up and down some hallway or staircase? What if I had to spend eternity reenacting my own death? Even if it were an exciting death, I'd get bored *very* quickly, and eternity is an awfully long time.

Even in a suburban town where the "historic district" is all of thirty or forty years old, kids will always make up ghost stories. In fact, one of the most notable supposedly haunted places in Urbandale was Merle Hay Mall, which was said to be built on the site of an old monastery. According to legend, the grounds were littered with the unmarked graves of monks, nuns, and the occasional miscarried fetus. The ghosts of these people could occasionally be seen wandering around, but the most talked-about spirit was the ghost of a nun who had killed herself when she became pregnant. The ghostly nun was said to carry a baby around the mall, weeping all the way.[1] A haunted mall—how suburban can you get?

But the local cemetery, where the grave of my elementary school's namesake could be seen from the road, was ground zero for ghosts in Urbandale. I would go to the haunted mall, but I wouldn't be caught dead (no pun intended) near a cemetery. Cemeteries freaked me out. I was never sure why they scared me so much, but it wasn't thoughts of women in white robes floating around that kept me up at night (not usually, anyway); it was dreams of rows and rows of gravestones.

The town graveyard was a small place, not much bigger than a backyard, called McDivitt Grove Cemetery. It wasn't the creepiest cemetery in the world; it wasn't very

---

1. Even when I was a kid, this story struck me as rather ridiculous. In the course of researching this book, I was rather shocked to find out that there actually *was* a monastery, a home to a sect of Passionist monks, on the site where the mall now stands. St. Gabriel's Monastery was built in the 1920s and closed in 1958 when the monks sold the land to the developers who built the mall. I don't know if there are really unmarked graves there, but it's hardly impossible. Certainly there have been strange things in the mall—when I was a kid, there was a seven-foot bronze statue of a naked guy with angel wings riding a tricycle outside of the bookstore. If you looked closely at his legs, there was some copper piping visible, as though the guy's innards were running hot and cold water. I never took much notice of the naked trike angel at the time, but now that I think back on it, it's no wonder that I grew up to be such a weirdo.

old and had no spooky statues or crypts. But it had the classic spooky wrought-iron gates with the name above the entrance. In a town made up mainly of newly built houses and an ever-expanding lineup of strip malls, this place seemed like a scene out of an old horror movie.

Closer to downtown Des Moines on University Street was the much larger Glendale Cemetery. It wasn't any spookier than McDivitt Grove (less so, if anything, since it lacked the spooky gates), but knowing I would be driving by it could worry me for days. It was a large enough cemetery that holding your breath while going past it—as all kids did when they were driven past it—was quite an athletic feat for a ten-year-old. I remember that there was a duck pond in the middle of it. I thought that those ducks were insane to hang around there.

Once I got to where I could hold my breath for the entire length of a car trip past Glendale, it didn't scare me as much. But McDivitt Grove continued to scare the crap out of me. Even though it was a good mile or so away from my house, I would occasionally get spooked just going into my basement on the grounds that I was probably just about eye-level with anything buried six feet under when I was down there.

In sixth grade, I started hanging out with a guy named Seth Kleinschrodt, and he and I became, all by ourselves, the Urbandale paranormal scene. We ran stakeouts at places we thought were haunted and went to every alien or monster movie that came out.

In those days, there were only a couple of shows about unexplained phenomena on television. There was *Sightings*, which I seem to recall aired only irregularly, and reruns of *In Search Of…* with Leonard Nimoy on A&E. So that was what we watched.

What impressed me about Seth was that the guy was fearless. He told me about a few ghost encounters he'd had himself—his house was certainly thought to be haunted. He talked of feeling "watched" there, and I felt as though I was, too. I can't remember *why* we thought it was haunted for the life of me. We had no information about anyone dying in the house or anything—it was Urbandale, Iowa, after all. Not enough people had died in town to fill up even a small cemetery like McDivitt Grove.

But, for one reason or another, Seth's place "felt" haunted. And Seth didn't seem to mind it. Ghost stories didn't keep him up at night—or, anyway, he said that they didn't. Maybe he just talked a good game.

Eventually, we hit on the idea of doing our own show, a public access TV program. Public access wasn't a very big deal in Des Moines—it only came on in the middle of the night. But we filmed a couple of episodes of *Strange Phenomena*, our own show, that I'm not entirely sure ever actually aired. The only thing I actually remember seeing on public access TV in Des Moines was a performance by a local heavy metal band called Modifidious. Still, I suppose making a public access TV show was a better way to pass the time than the other popular local pastime, which was crystal meth. Even the cop who taught our "drug abuse resistance" classes turned out to be selling meth.

My fear of cemeteries followed me all through my youth. When I was about fifteen, my family moved to suburban Atlanta, which was chock full of old graveyards—some Southern Baptists believe that bodies have to be buried in consecrated ground on the church property, so every church in town (and there were a *lot* of churches in town) came complete with its own little graveyard.

One day, shortly after we moved, I saw an episode of *Sightings* (or some other such show; the surprise popularity of *The X-Files* had led to there being a few more of them by then) about the famous ghost of a girl people met in Chicago dance halls. They would offer to drive her home, intending, surely, to get a quick shag in on the way, only to have her vanish outside of a cemetery.

I'd heard variations of the story before, of course—vanishing hitchhikers are a common ghost story. People a bit older than me were pretty generally introduced to the vanishing hitchhiker story by the song "Strange Things Happen in This World" by Dickie Betts. People about my age or younger know it from a variation told in the book *In a Dark, Dark Room and Other Scary Stories* by Alvin Schwartz, which has long been a staple of Easy Reader libraries. I'd heard several versions of the story by then, so I don't know what it was about that TV show, but it scared me out of my wits.

The next night, while driving around, my dad took a wrong turn, and we ended up on something called "Cemetery Road" out in the middle of a dark, dark woods. I was so spooked that I didn't really recover for a couple of weeks.

When I started driving myself, I would drive a long way out of my way to avoid going past any graveyards. Honestly, I probably have to take a small chunk of the blame for global warming personally, given how many miles out of my way I drove to keep from going past graveyards when I was seventeen or eighteen.

But it all stopped, rather abruptly, when I was about twenty. I think it started to go away the day we went to Westminster Abbey when my family went to England to visit some relatives who were living there. At the time, I hadn't actually been *in* a cemetery in years and years. I was nervous about going there, since the Abbey is really nothing but an indoor graveyard; you can sit down on what you think is a bench and realize that you're actually parking your ass on the Earl of Southampton's coffin. But I wasn't about to mess up the family vacation due to a childhood phobia.

After a couple of minutes of deep breathing and tension in the Abbey, I started to calm down. The fact that I was staring down a coffin containing the very dust and bones that had been Queen Elizabeth wasn't so scary after all. In fact, it was fascinating.

I had faced my fear. When I got back home, cemeteries just didn't seem to bother me as much any more. I even went inside of a couple of them voluntarily. The town I was living in at the time, Carrolton, had a very old, lovely cemetery in the middle of town. Interestingly, there was an adjacent swimming pool that had a water slide that was bordered on three sides by the cemetery. A cemetery that appears to have a water slide in the middle of it is not a sight to be missed.

A couple of years later, I moved to Milledgeville, Georgia, to finish college. The first thing I did upon moving there was to ask a longtime resident what all of the local ghost stories were. By this time, I had grown a lot more skeptical—genuinely skeptical, not just telling myself I was a skeptic to keep from getting scared. People would tell me about UFOs or surviving dinosaurs or ghosts, and I'd sort of roll my eyes. I figured that maybe I had just gotten it all out of my system when I was a kid, and these people (who all would have thought I was a nerd for talking about the Loch Ness Monster when I was ten) were just discovering strange phenomena.

But ghost stories are just as much a part of any town as the "real" local history. Whether or not they're true doesn't matter a bit. Knowing all of the local legends is a great way to familiarize yourself with a new town.

So my friend Mandy took me on a tour of haunted Milledgeville. This was the first town I'd lived in that was in no way a suburb—it was just a small town in the middle of nowhere. And, quite unlike most of the other towns in which I'd lived, the place was old and full of history. Prior to the Civil War, it had served as the state capitol. The old governor's mansion, which briefly served as General Sherman's headquarters, stood on the college campus. For some reason, it was painted a shade of pink. I liked to imagine Sherman marching up and thinking, *Well, no wonder we kicked their asses!*

The mansion was supposed to be haunted, of course. Almost all historical mansions are. There were also rumors that there was, at least at one point, a tunnel from the mansion to the old capitol building a few blocks away that could be used as an escape route. Tunnel rumors are common in just about any old town, really. And many of them actually turn out to be true.

Just west of downtown stood the Walker house, a gothic revival mansion once owned by Old Man Walker, the Meanest Man in Town. According to the stories, when his son was sent home from college during a flu epidemic, Old Man Walker insisted his son was faking it and put him to work in the field. When the son collapsed, he shut him in his room and forbid the servants to tend to him. The son wandered out of the room, dizzy and delirious, probably looking for water, and fell down the stairs to his death. The house is now haunted either by a grieving Mr. Walker or his unfortunate son, depending on who's telling the story. Others say it's haunted by Mr. Walker's wife, whom he also apparently killed. I had my doubts about the story, but just knowing it made me feel a connection to the town. Eventually, knowing the old legends was about the *only* thing that made me feel connected to that little town, where I didn't really fit in.

By this time, I was over my fear of cemeteries enough that I even let Mandy take me around Memory Hill, the old town graveyard. It's a gorgeous old graveyard, full of odd and interesting things. The most famous ghost there is probably in a hillside crypt known as the Fish Tomb. The story goes that one day Mr. Fish, devastated over the loss of his wife, crawled into the crypt and shot himself in the head—they say you can still sometimes hear the gunshot if you knock on the door of the crypt.

"Do you believe in ghosts?" Mandy asked as we stood before the Fish Tomb.

"Nah," I said.

"Care to knock on the door, then?" she asked.

"Nope." I said. I was skeptical, but not above being scared. And, anyway, triggering some ghost to relive the moment of its suicide wouldn't be very nice, now, would it?

Elsewhere in the graveyard is the grave of a supposed witch, the grave of author Flannery O'Connor, and a statue that's supposed to be of the Virgin Mary but looks for all the world like George Washington in a dress to me. It's a pretty terrific place.

The cemetery didn't spook me at all. But then there was the abandoned mental hospital—that was another story.

You just don't hear about abandoned mental hospitals that *aren't* supposed to be haunted. Sitting on the outskirts of town, Central State Hospital was once the largest mental hospital in the world. Back in the nineteenth century, it was known as the Georgia Lunatic Asylum. One can only imagine what kind of horrible things went on in there back in the days when electroshock therapy and lobotomies were all the rage. The rumors about what went on there were probably nothing compared to what actually happened. As a lasting testament to what kind of a place it was, there is a small monument set up to honor the twenty-five thousand or so unmarked graves that are known to be on the grounds. The hospital is still in operation—Mandy actually worked there at the time—but several of the buildings are long abandoned.

The place spooked me good. Everything about it freaked me out. The sheer air around the place felt heavy and haunted. Every time I went near there, I felt as though I were being watched by unseen eyes, followed by silent footsteps.

And I went back several times. I had to. The best job I could find in town was delivering pizza, which was a really tricky job in a town like Milledgeville. Outside of the leafy town square, with its mansions and columns, the town was just one ghetto after another. Street signs tended to go missing, and the houses and trailers tended to be unnumbered. Finding addresses involved a lot of tricky detective work in spooky old neighborhoods, escapes from unfriendly dogs, and occasional encounters with large groups of unfriendly teenagers.

Frequently, I would have to take pizzas out to the mental hospital. Sometimes they would tell me which building I was to go to, and other times the address simply read "Central State Hospital," which meant that it could go to any of the handful of buildings that were still in operation, leaving me to explore the place on a mad quest to figure out who had ordered a pizza. None of the people who ordered pizza there, for the record, ever tipped. This was par for the course in the town, though. I averaged about ten cents per delivery on Friday nights.

But if the job didn't pay much in terms of money, it paid in stories. I got to explore the darkest, spookiest corners of the town. I found out more than I'd ever known about how to get into a prison on a guest pass (there were seven or eight prisons in town). I learned where the whorehouses were and where to go if I ever decided to embark on a career as a crackhead (which, funnily enough, were the same place). And, every now and then, I'd get to see the insides of the old mansions that were supposed to be haunted.

Skeptical though I was, I still got spooked every now and then. But the job toughened me up; if I hadn't done it, I don't know if I ever would have had what it takes to become a professional ghostbuster a couple of years later.

After earning my ever-useful degree in English, I moved to Chicago. Moving there had been my main goal in life ever since I'd gone there for a Tom Waits concert my first week of college. Atlanta had never grown on me; it's the sort of town where one has to drive a long way to get anywhere, the streets snake around every which way, and there aren't many old buildings. They tend to tear things down every twenty years or so there. Atmosphere is in short supply, as the strip malls and Super Walmarts gradually take over the suburbs and ever-expanding exurbs and make the towns seem more and more like airports. Plus, it almost never snowed, and summer seemed to last nine months. This is a selling point for some people, but I missed the four-season Midwest.

Chicago was like a paradise to me. I still tend to shrug off stories of mystical energies, but something about the city had just called to me. The streets were on an easy-to-navigate grid system. The buildings were old and cool. There was no need even to own a car. In my first apartment, I almost never needed to go more than three miles from home. My parents had to drive about three miles just to get a container of milk in suburban Atlanta.

Of course, as soon as I got to town, I asked a lifelong resident what some of the local ghost stories were. And the first one I was told about was of Resurrection Mary, the town's vanishing hitchhiker. As soon as I heard the story, I recognized it—it was the exact ghost I'd seen that TV show about years earlier. The one that left me spooked for weeks. But it didn't spook me quite as much anymore.

I was hardened by years of delivering pizza to haunted houses.

Now, one thing my generation got really screwed on was college; we all grew up believing that if we got good grades and went to college, we'd get a good job. Having some experience working at restaurants, grocery stores, and other such typical high school jobs would make us even more attractive to employers. It was true for our parents. It was probably true as recently as a decade or so ago. Employers would look at your resumé and say, "Yeah, you seem like a smart, hardworking fellow. I'm sure you could handle this job."

But that isn't the way it turned out for my generation—employers don't look for college degrees anymore. All that they want is three years of experience in a specific field. I never got a job because of my degree, and I can't think of anyone my age who did. A business degree today isn't any less useless than a philosophy degree. Hell, I could have quit school in seventh grade and compiled a nasty police record, and it wouldn't have made me any less employable than I was after college.

I tried to find work in some industry other than retail and restaurant work, but the few employers who would interview me looked at my resumé and said I didn't have the necessary experience for an entry-level job, then asked if I'd thought of applying at the new Starbucks that was opening in the lobby. Most of the people who *did* want to interview me turned out to be pyramid schemers, and even a couple of *those* turned me down.

So I worked in a handful of wretchedly bad restaurants, put in a tour of duty (my fourth) at Starbucks, and lugged boxes in the back of several department stores for only nominally more money than I'd made bagging groceries at fourteen.

In June of 2005, my first summer in Chicago, my first young-adult novel, How to Get Suspended and Influence People, sold to Random House, which helped me immensely, but didn't pay enough that I could quit my myriad day jobs. I was going to have to keep living the life of a McHobo (one who bums from nametag job to nametag job) a little while longer.

A few months after the book sold, I was starving my way through the months between tourist season and the holidays, which are lonely months for McHobos. One night, a help-wanted ad for Chicago Spooks, a ghost tour company, appeared online.

I figured it was a long shot—who wouldn't want a job that cool?—but sent in a resumé anyway, and, to my great surprise, I got an interview. I was to go along on the tour and meet Ken, who was the main guide at the time.

I showed up at the pickup spot outside of the McDonald's on Clark Street early—it was a pleasant walk from my apartment—and Ken arrived with the bus at about half past six.

I'd been on an awful lot of job interviews since I'd moved to the city. They were all the same—some assistant manager-type would ask me about crap like "leadership skills" and other management-speak gobbledygook that had very little to do with waiting tables or pouring coffee. So when Ken asked me to tell him about myself, I started in with a bit about my experience in public speaking, writing, and stuff like that.

"Don't worry about that stuff," he said, with a dismissive wave of his hand. "What do you know about ghosts?"

Right then, I told myself that if I screwed this one up, I'd never, ever forgive myself.

I told him I knew the basic theories about ghosts and other weird stuff; that I was always the kid in school who was never seen without a book about the Loch Ness Monster under his arm. And I told him that I was pretty skeptical about ghosts.

"That's fine," he said. "We all are. But it's all about how much you know. Do you know what an orb is?"

"Sure," I said. "It's a little white ball of light that shows up in pictures. Some people say they're ghosts, but they're probably just dew points or something."

"What if we can run tests to show there's not enough moisture in the air?" asked Ken.

"Well, I guess there's a lot of stuff that could explain it," I said. "Dust, light refraction. Stuff like that."

I guess this answer was good enough for Ken.

I'd seen hundreds of orb pictures—a lot of ghost websites displayed them and held them up as "proof" that a place was haunted. Some said they were the most basic form of spirit energy. I'd never been that impressed with them, myself. Few real ghost hunters are. Even if they *are* ghosts, a ball of light just isn't as cool as a transparent woman in white.

I proceeded to tell him about the "ghost picture" that had been taken of me on Liberty Street in Milledgeville. Liberty was a street that ran from the prison (on the site where the college now stands) to the cemetery and was so known because taking that road was the only way the prisoners would ever be free. One night, I was doing a photo shoot dressed as Oliver Twist (for reasons I no longer recall) to promote a new album I'd recorded with my band. In two of the shots in front of an old mansion, a few doors from the graveyard, I was surrounded by blobs of strange, misty lights. I put them online, with a link to an article debunking such blobs as little more than digital cameras reacting badly to low light—an article that, it turned out, was written by Troy Taylor, who was running the business end of Chicago Spooks at the time. If I got the job, he'd be my boss.

There were only three people on the tour that night— fairly typical for a freezing November evening just before the Thanksgiving holidays. As we took off, I sat back to watch and observe while Ken regaled the three tourists with stories. I was a little bit nervous—as a skeptic, could I tell tourists that a place was haunted in good conscience? Would I have to make myself look like a flake? Would looking like a flake be bad for my career as a writer?

Ken explained that the reason Chicago was so haunted was probably that it was situated next to Lake Michigan. Most of the cities with a reputation for being haunted—London, Edinburgh, San Francisco, St. Augustine, Savannah, etc.—tend to be located near major bodies of water. The reason for this, he explained, is that moisture is a conductor of electricity, and ghosts seem to use electricity to manifest. Haunted locations tend to have lots of strange electromagnetic field readings, cold spots (little localized areas that are noticeably cooler than they ought to be) are reported frequently, and sudden battery drainage is a common problem.

As a skeptic, this explanation sort of appealed to me. I'd always wondered if ghosts might just be a scientific phenomenon waiting to be explained. Even the most hardened skeptic ought to be able to admit that there are oddities in the environment, such as weird electrical effects here and there. Whether they actually come from dead people or not, or whether they have any strange reactions to ghostly energies that allow them to "manifest," they can at least have the psychological effect of making people *feel* as though there's a dead person around. Going along with my theory that it all comes down to semantics, any place where people are likely to *think* there's a ghost around can be considered haunted for all practical purposes. This helped with my moral dilemma quite a bit.

I was further helped when Ken said, "Let me explain to everyone a bit about what I do as a psychic. No, I can't read your mind, I didn't predict 9/11, and I don't know the lottery numbers. If I did, do you really think I'd be here running ghost tours? I'd be on a beach someplace, drinking a mai tai! What I have is just really good instincts. By having me on a ghost investigation, I can tell people where to look, and that cuts down the time an investigation takes just about in half." Even as a skeptic, his psychic talk didn't make me roll my eyes one bit. Some people *do* have better instincts than others, after all. Like so many things, whether this counts as psychic ability really just comes down to semantics.

The first stop that night was at the site of the Iroquois Theater, where the deadliest single-building fire in U.S. history occurred in 1903. From there, we proceeded up through Lincoln Park, the site of the old City Cemetery (and still home to upwards of twenty thousand bodies that weren't moved along with their tombstones), past the tomb of Ira Couch (the last remaining crypt from City Cemetery), and up to a little field that was once the site of SMC Cartage Company, where Al Capone had seven gangsters lined up against the wall and shot in a coup that came to be known as the St. Valentine's Day Massacre.

Ken was a fantastic tour guide. My initial worries that he was going to be a New Age wacko—he *did* tell me he was a professional psychic right off the bat—were swept away quickly. He was informative and witty, and about 90 percent of the tour was strictly historically based. Ken, in fact, was pretty up-front about saying that even though the St. Valentine's Day Massacre site was rumored to be haunted, he didn't think it was actually haunted at all. He told us the ghost stories that went around about it, but he said that the stories about it were probably just made up by other ghost tour guides (with help from this old drunk who lives in the senior apartments next door and occasionally hangs around outside, harassing passers-by) as an excuse to go there. It's a common thing on ghost tours—lots of ghost tours look at a historical spot, say "Wouldn't it be cool if *that* were haunted?" and make up a ghost story to go with it. I knew enough about history to know that Ken wasn't letting facts get in the way of a good story at a couple of stops, but he wasn't bullshitting me nearly as much as I'd expected.

After the Capone story, we stopped in for a quick drink at a nearby bar (a former speakeasy). There, we all sat around a small table, chatting. This, I decided, was my chance to show Ken what I could do.

I managed to tell a couple of Milledgeville ghost stories, including one about a girl who, years before, had hanged herself in the top floor of one of the dorm buildings as the soldier who had gotten her pregnant marched by in a parade outdoors. Today, that floor is shut down and locked.

"Is that true?" asked Ken.

"Well, sort of," I said. "The suicide story is apparently true, but the reason the place is closed down isn't ghosts. There's just a lot of asbestos up there."

I then managed to work in the story of the Glowing Grave, a grave in a downtown Des Moines cemetery that had a tendency to glow. The story went that the man buried there had lived across the street from the cemetery with his wife, and, on his death, he warned her not to remarry and that he'd be watching her from the grave—hence the glow.

"Did you ever go out there?" Ken asked.

"Sure," I lied. I wouldn't have actually gone out to a graveyard in my Iowa days for anything. "I'm pretty sure it just glows because of a streetlight near it."

"That's *usually* what it is," Ken admitted.

The tour continued through Cabrini-Green, the rundown projects that were said to be the home of the Candyman, and up to the site of the *Eastland* disaster, a haunted stretch of the Chicago River. From there we swung down to the Jane Addams Hull House on South Halsted, which I'd read about many times before. It had a long-standing reputation for being a particularly haunted place—and, in the cold, dark night, it *was* a pretty spooky-looking old mansion.

I guess that my attempts to tell a few ghost stories at the bar had been successful, because at the end of the tour, Ken told me the job was mine if I wanted it. Ken and I had hit it off right away, because we were both geeks. I caught all of his references to H. P. Lovecraft, whose works I'd discovered way back when I was in junior high school. And I guess his psychic instincts told him that I'd be a good tour guide.

"Now that you've been on the tour," he said, "does it seem like something you'd want to do?"

"Hell yeah," I said.

"Awesome," said Ken. "We'll have to get approval from Olga, of course, but as far as I'm concerned, the job is yours." I later found out that he'd called Olga and said, "He's perfect! He looks just like Harry Potter!"

A few days later, I spoke to Olga on the phone, and we chatted amiably for a bit. She assured me that she was a skeptic, too, but said that, on investigations, "We try to keep a sense of wonder."

So she offered me the job—not only would I be running the tours from time to time, I'd also be expected to come along on ghost investigations now and then. I'd officially traded in my Starbucks apron for a job as a ghostbuster.

There was one hitch: I still insisted, at least to myself, that there was no such thing as ghosts. But this job would start me off on a long journey to a lot of questions.

What are ghosts, anyway? Are they *all* just figments of the imagination? Can a sudden, traumatic death "create" a ghost? Could science explain this, or is it all in the realm of the "supernatural?"

These questions have been going around for centuries, and we're no closer to an answer now than we ever were.

Working with Ghosts

There's really no single way to do a ghost tour. There are lots of them around the world, and all of them are different. Some are really corny spook shows with a lot of special effects, some are pretty bare-bones. Some are rooted in historical stories, others focus more on local legends, and others just make stuff up altogether. Recently, more and more have been letting customers use electromagnetic field readers and other gear and have actually taken them ghost hunting (though few, if any, show people how to use the gear correctly).

Any given tour could vary greatly depending on who the guide was. After that first tour with Ken, I rode along on one of the tours run by Chris Thieme, a ghost hunter who occasionally worked as a tour guide for the company. His tour went to most of the same places as Ken's, but the tour itself was completely different. He was a lot more sedate than Ken and told a few different stories. He didn't talk much about ghosts or science—he was more focused on history and stuck closer to the facts than Ken did. His jokes were generally cornier, too. I kept careful notes, making sure to get all of the right names, dates, and body counts.

A few weeks later, when I went along on a second tour with Ken, he told me he was going to have me handle most of the work that particular night. I just about panicked—I'd been doing my homework, all right, but I certainly wasn't ready to run a tour by myself.

But there's only one way to learn to do a tour, and that's to be thrown in headfirst, as Ken did to me. I won't say that I did a good job that night—in fact, I stunk. I stumbled over names and dates, and my jokes fell flat.

"You're actually doing great," Ken told me when we stopped at the Clark Bar. "Most of this stuff you'll pick up as you go along. The most important thing right now is to slow down. You're talking too fast."

This was especially driven home at the next stop, the site of the *Eastland* disaster.

In 1915, the Western Electric Company booked the *Eastland*, a steamer known as the Speed Queen of the Great Lakes, to take their employees on a picnic. They were to be picked up in the Chicago River between Clark and LaSalle, sail across Lake Michigan, and have a picnic on the dunes of Michigan City, Indiana.

The trip was a disaster (hence the term *Eastland disaster*). The ship was overloaded with passengers, the new concrete deck and lifeboats made the boat top-heavy, and there were problems with the ballast system. Through a huge confluence of bad luck and mismanagement, the ship actually tipped over, coming to rest on its side in the Chicago River. People below deck were crushed to death by falling furniture or were unable to swim out of the boat when the water rushed in. People above deck were thrown overboard—most of them couldn't swim, and most were wearing the heavy fashions that people wore in 1915. Once you got those kind of clothes wet, you might as well have been wearing an anchor.

I tried to slow down my cadence at that spot—I really did. But I still told the story of the *Eastland* entirely too quickly. When we got off the bus to look for ghosts, Ken told me that I had to kill about twenty minutes out there on the river, rather than the usual five to ten.

"Don't worry," he said. "I have a plan." And he led the entire group down the steps to the little sidewalk area that went along the river.

"Are there any Pisces women here?" he asked. A couple of women raised their hands.

"All right," he said. "There's a ghost of a boy here who died along with his mother, and he tends to latch onto Pisces women, since his mother was a Pisces. What I want you each to do is walk from where we're standing down the end of the sidewalk and back. Pay close attention to what you feel and what you hear on each side of you."

Both women slowly ambled down the sidewalk and came back—both saying that they had heard vague voices coming from the water and felt as though a small boy were trying to grab at their hands.

I was pretty impressed. I was skeptical enough to assume that the reason they'd felt all of that was that Ken had sort of psychologically set them up for it, but it worked, and it killed time.

But it wouldn't work for me. I couldn't possibly make any pretense of knowing the first thing about astrology, and I couldn't lay claim to being a psychic, the way Ken could.

"Don't worry," said Ken, as we walked back to the bus. "As you come here more often and learn more stuff, you'll learn plenty of ways to stretch the time out if you have to. There's also supposed to be a ghost of a guy who hanged himself that you can see in a window of the building across the river. If all else fails, you can just have them stare at the window for a while."

I doubted a lot of the stories—certainly I never found any reason to believe a guy had hanged himself in front of that window. But eventually I came to realize that it didn't really matter—there didn't necessarily need to be actual ghosts at a place to make it haunted. If the locations were said to be haunted, that *made* them haunted in a very real way.

In 1990, Helen Ackley of Nyack, New York, put her Victorian home on the market for $650,000, intending to sell it and move to Florida. The place was often noted for looking like the house from *The Munsters*. She eventually sold the place to a couple who paid her a $32,000 down payment. A few months later, the buyers sued her for the return of the down payment on the grounds that she had not disclosed the fact that the house was haunted prior to the sale.

In fact, Ackley had been advertising the place as a haunted house for years, and it had built up quite a reputation. She had reported seeing several apparitions walking around the place, including one of a guy that appeared to be from the Revolutionary War era (which, of course, would be a bit out of place in a Victorian house, seeing as how it wouldn't have been built until decades after the revolution). It had been written up in *Reader's Digest* and was regularly included on ghost tours of Nyack. Ghost hunters showed up from time to time to poke around.

This had the two buyers rather miffed—one was just plain annoyed by the house having such a reputation, and the other was downright scared to live in a haunted house. When Ackley refused to give the deposit back, they took her to court. Eventually, the case went all the way to the New York Supreme Court.

In a three-two decision, the court ruled in the buyer's favor—the "haunting," whatever the real cause of it, was a pre-existing condition that should have been disclosed.

Whether there were actually any ghosts floating around the place or not, the buyers were going to have to deal with ghost hunters and tours showing up from time to time, and the house's reputation might make it less marketable should they decide to resell it.

I, for one, might dispute the idea that a supposedly haunted place is less marketable. In the course of my work, I've met plenty of people who would probably pay extra for the chance to live in a haunted house. But the decision of the court stood. In his decision, Justice Stevens, who presided over the case, wrote, "Whether the source of the spectral apparitions seen by defendant seller is parapsychic or psychogenic, having reported their presence in both a national publication and the local press, defendant is estopped to deny their existence and, as a matter of law, the house is haunted." Ever since, house sellers in New York have been required by law to report supposed hauntings as a pre-existing condition. Connecticut quickly passed a similar law.

So I was willing, even in my skepticism, to go ahead and call places "haunted." Eventually, I hit on the strategy of never telling people—or myself—that there actually *was* a ghost in any particular location. After telling the history of the place, I would simply tell the passengers on the bus what people had *claimed* to see there, and, after I'd spent enough time there myself, what I'd seen there. And I reminded myself that people didn't come on ghost tours for scientific explanations and debunking—they came for thrills and chills. If they wanted me to get all skeptical, they could e-mail me after the tour.

Eventually, in fact, I took it for granted that some of the places *were* haunted. I didn't know *what* was haunting them, or how. Was there really a dead person there? Was it just some sort of leftover energy, someone experiencing the afterlife, or just a weird environmental effect?

I eventually hit on an easy way to deal with these questions: just not worrying about them. There was *something* weird about the places, something that, at the very least, made people *think* there was a dead guy—or dead guys—hanging around there. Exactly what the nature of the haunting was didn't really matter. It would matter if I wanted to hold up these spots as proof of the afterlife, but, well, I didn't.

A couple of months after I was hired came my first solo tour. Troy arranged for my driver that day to be Hector, an improv comic who had been a driver for the company for some time. He knew the tour backward and forward and could take over for me if I got into trouble.

Hector, a bearded Latin-American guy, arrived with the bus that night, ushered me into a nearby gas station to grab a bottle of water, then gave me some friendly advice.

"The important thing," he said, "is to have a good time. If you have a good time, they'll have a good time. That's what it's all about. And let me know if you run into trouble. I'll help out."

I came to realize that Hector was never one to shy away from helping out—or taking any opportunity to grab the microphone.

I didn't do so well that first night. I realized, midway through the tour, that I'd already used the phrase "as the years went by" about a dozen times. The biggest problem, though—one that I couldn't have possibly helped—was that, being new to the route, I wasn't yet familiar with exactly how long it would take to get from point A to point B, and, therefore, I didn't know exactly how long to make each story. I could tell the Navy Pier story and still have several blocks of Lake Shore Drive to travel down before we got to City Cemetery. This left me with some uncomfortable silences.

"Well," I said into the mic, "does anyone here live in a haunted house?" I'd seen Ken ask this question a couple of times. Usually, someone would tell about a spooky old house where they used to live where the doors opened and closed on their own or something like that.

No one raised their hand.

Except for Hector.

"All right," I said. "Then I cede the mic to Hector."

Hector took the mic—while driving—and told about a ghost he had seen in his old apartment. He had been washing dishes, which he had allowed to pile up for entirely too long, and looked around behind him to see a little girl in an old-fashioned dress and black shoes. She was pointing at him. Scariest of all, though, was that she had no face.

"The next thing I remember," Hector said, "I had run all the way to the grocery store four blocks away. Barefoot. And when I got back, the dishes were all clean."

"Well, that's handy," I said, taking the mic back. "I wouldn't mind having a ghost do my dishes for me."

"You would if she didn't have a face!" said Hector. And he shivered.

I assumed—though he always insisted otherwise—that he was making the story up. Ghosts like that normally only seem to show up in movies. I've never met a ghost hunter with a story quite like that; most of the more reputable ones, in fact, will claim that they've only seen a ghost once or twice, if at all, and then only in fleeting glimpses. But it was a good story—and it got us the rest of the way to City Cemetery.

The tour wasn't great—I felt as though I was really tanking. Eventually, I fell back on using bad jokes—most of which I'd taken from Ken's and Chris's tours.

"Now," I said as we passed the site of the old O'Leary Barn where the Chicago fire started in 1872, "we no longer blame the great Chicago fire on Mrs. O'Leary's cow."

"The whole Mrs. O'Leary thing came from an anti-Irish newspaper," said Hector. "It was called *The Chicago Tribune*."

"That's right," I said, moving into Chris's worst joke. "In 1997, the city actually even issued an apology to Mrs. O'Leary and her cow. Because, as you know, to err is human, and to forgive, bovine."

The crowd tittered.

"Man," said Hector, "I'm gonna kill that Chris Thieme."

After the tour that night, Hector assured me that my tour was perfectly solid—no one would be complaining or anything—but that I'd need to loosen up a bit.

And the next night, I did. When we got to Lake Shore Drive, I had Hector tell the same story about the girl without a face.

"So there I was," he said, "finally getting around to the dishes. And I look around, and there's this little girl in a blue dress, standing in the doorway, and pointing at me."

"And it's not polite to point," I said. I'd been planning that one. The crowd snickered a bit.

"That's right," said Hector. "But scariest of all—and this is what kept me up all night for days—was that she had no face. Just a blank space where her face should have been."

I snatched the mic back.

"You see," I said. "Most ghosts don't really even seem to know that they're there—they're just sort of like video recordings that play over and over again. But every now and then, we do run into a ghost that seems to be trying to communicate with us. In this case, the ghost was pointing at Hector to say, 'You, sir, are a slob!'"

"It's true," said Hector, nodding, as people chuckled. "I am."

But I wasn't finished.

"'In fact,'" I said, using my spookiest "ghostly little girl" voice, "'you are such a slob that I can't even show my face in this joint!'"

This caught Hector, and everyone else, off-guard. This time, the people didn't titter, they actually laughed. Hard. So did Hector.

"Well played!" he said, nodding at me approvingly.

That was my first really good tour. I'd worked a lot of jobs in my day—just a *lot* of jobs. The notion that I might actually be *good* at one of them was a whole new feeling for me. I made up my mind that I was going to give the best tours in the city.

Outside of research and experience, the main thing I needed to learn was the nuances of the route—how long each story should take and where to tell what story. For instance, I had to learn exactly when to start telling the story of Resurrection Mary and how to vary the story based on whether the traffic lights were red or green so that I'd be just at the right part in the story when we reached the 'L' track support beam where Mary Bregovy, one of the girls sometimes said to be the girl who became the ghost, was killed. And how long to continue the story after that so that it ended just before we got to Harpo Studios.

The Mary story *had* to end by then—for one thing, it's impossible to hold tourists' attention with a ghost story when they're suddenly going by Harpo Studios, home of the Oprah show, and partly because there was a ghost story *about* the studios that I had to tell. In 1915, the building had been the Second Regiment Armory building, where about five hundred of the bodies of the victims of the *Eastland* disaster were brought until they could be identified. Several ghosts have since been rumored to haunt the place, including a ghostly woman in a long gray dress who floats down one of the hallways. She's usually known as the Gray Lady, although I like to call her the Phantom of the Oprah.

Soon, Hector and I had developed a regular two-step routine in which I was the straight man. I'd tell a story, and he'd throw in a joke. I'd tell a bad joke, and he'd tell a worse one. And, though I wasn't about to tell people there was a "portal" in the garden next to Hull House that led to the netherworld, even though that sort of thing was what some people wanted to hear, Hector had no problem with it. The tours we gave together were excellent.

Ken and Hector didn't get along that well—they were friends, but in a brotherly way. They picked on each other constantly. To a person looking at them from the middle (me), it was rather funny. Still, since they tended to argue, Hector normally didn't drive on Ken's tours. Ken used Willie, a much quieter driver who wouldn't dream of interrupting.

Ken and Willie had a routine of their own. To understand it, you have to realize that a great many of our customers were tourists who were a little bit scared to be in the city—their minds were filled with stories about muggers, drive-bys, and gangs, none of which were much in evidence anywhere near the tourist area. Gangs don't

Willie

spend a lot of time fighting for control of the Rainforest Cafe.

Anyway, Ken usually drove the bus downtown himself—they kept it parked near his house—and met Willie there. He'd be bantering with early-bird customers when Willie, a black guy in a hooded sweatshirt, arrived.

"Got any change?" Willie would ask.

"Oh no," Ken would say. "Not you again! Listen, buddy, I know you need two bucks for diapers for your baby or whatever, but the answer is no!"

"I don't need no diapers for my baby," said Willie, as he pushed his way aboard. "I need new uniforms for my soccer team! And some crack!"

"Well," Ken would say, "if you want any cash, we're gonna put you to work! You know how to drive a bus?"

"I think so," Willie would say. "I've seen it on TV. This button makes it go, right?"

"Good enough," Ken would reply. "Get onboard! You're driving tonight!"

"Okay," said Willie. "But I'm gonna need some heroin first."

I'm not sure that this routine actually scared anyone, but it amused Ken and Willie to no end.

Even if they didn't scare anybody, a few people probably at least believed that Willie was a panhandler at first—there were plenty of people circulating the area asking for money in exchange for any number of strange goods and services. We took to calling them "Jawas," after the guys who roam around in *Star Wars* selling broken droids and other junk. Our favorite was a particularly odd-looking fellow who was always trying to sell gold necklaces. We nicknamed him Fagin. One of the more honest fellows solicited donations for "Jack Daniel's Research." Another favorite of mine—the only one I ever actually gave any money to—was a shoeshiner who took his work awfully seriously. "I don't shine your shoes!" he claimed as he worked. "I make love to your feet!" And he did.

It wasn't always easy work—occasionally I'd get a school group full of kids who just weren't that bright. Even more often, I'd get groups of adults who just weren't that bright. These made for rough work, because I constantly had to think ahead to see if there was a joke or a big word coming up that the people on the bus might not understand. It's amazing how many people don't know the word "gallows."

Then, of course, we had the drunks. My years in restaurants had given me very, very strong feelings about obnoxious drunks. I'm not a violent sort of guy; the last fight I got in was a shoving match in seventh grade, and I probably would have lost it if a teacher hadn't broken it up. But there is something about an obnoxious drunk that just brings out every single violent instinct in my body.

When you work at restaurants, management tells you over and over during training to cut people off if they seem even tipsy, but in practice, you're never actually allowed to do it. Some waiters are afraid to cut people off, since they know they aren't going to get a tip if they do, and most managers won't back you up on it anyway. If you try to cut people off, they'll ask to see the manager, who will apologize on your behalf and buy them a beer.

On the tours, we'd occasionally get people who thought that going on a ghost tour was a good excuse to get trashed and act like jerks. October was especially bad for this; I sometimes wonder if the same drunks who crowd onto ghost tours close to Halloween are the terrors of the Christmas hayride industry. But I hit on a fine way of dealing with them. If anyone got too out of line, I'd drop them off somewhere and leave them there. In a bad neighborhood, if I could arrange it. I didn't have a manager looking over my shoulder, ready to take the drunk's side, so I reasoned that I didn't have to put up with anyone I didn't want to. It was a good feeling.

But if people showed up wanting a really good tour, not just an excuse to get trashed, they'd get it. Between the four of us—Ken, Hector, Willie, and I—we were giving the best tours in the city, if I do say so myself. Not just the best ghost tours, either—the best tours, period. My goal was that people would go home and not shut up about the tour for weeks—and, based on the letters I got, I was fairly successful.

The tour became different depending on the crowd. With some groups—the ones who seemed smart or at least like they took history seriously—I would go out of my way to get the facts right. On some groups I had to—every now and then we'd get a historian who was just itching to correct me any time I got a date wrong. With other groups, though, it seemed that most of the people didn't know Al Capone from Al Sharpton. With these people, I didn't feel bad about making stuff up, since they were unlikely to remember the details anyway.

The really tricky nights were when half of the crowd just wanted to drink, and half of the crowd just wanted to see haunted places. There were basically three kinds of crowds:

1. The kind that wanted to hear a ghost story about Navy Pier, the pier where Chicago keeps its tourists, when we drove past it.

2. The kind that would have preferred to hear me joke that the Ferris wheel at Navy Pier was actually not a Ferris wheel, but the world's largest statue of an anus. Why some of these people come on a ghost tour at all is sometimes beyond me—quite a few times, these sorts of people have come up to me halfway through and said, "Jeez, man, how come all these stories are about dead people?"

3. A mix of the two. Usually, the people who want to know about ghosts and history and the people who just want jokes and booze get along, and the tours become a mix to please both. Other times, it's a bit harder, since some people want nothing but pub stops and the others want nothing but ghosts. So people will complain no matter where I go or what I say. In these cases, I play to the ghost crowd, not the drinkers. Even the spookiest version of the tour has to have plenty of jokes, after all, so the customers who don't really care about the stories should still be entertained.

Usually, the people in the crowd who didn't really care about the stories, but just wanted to scream out the window now and then, would start to accept the tour for what it was, and even get into it after a stop or two. Telling the stories well was crucial, but orb pictures helped a lot. A couple of good orb pictures early in the tour could make even the more difficult drinkers forget about drinking and spend the rest of the night trying to get more ghost pictures.

As skeptical as I was about orbs—even Hector, who was their biggest supporter on the tours, called them a "parlor trick" in private—I grew to like them a bit. I even looked into getting a camera that was susceptible to false positives, just to liven things up on slow nights. Getting good orb pictures was fairly common in Death Alley, the first major stop of the tour. "I can't really analyze it based on the LCD screen," I'd say when someone got an orb shot on a digital camera, "but that's exactly what orbs look like!" Getting a possible ghost picture on the first stop was a great way to get people excited early on, no matter how much time I spent explaining that almost all orb pictures could be explained away pretty easily. I told people straight up that even when we get orbs we can't explain, it's a major leap to say, "It's not dust, so it must be a dead person." If anyone got really freaked out when orbs showed up in pictures (and many people did), I'd say, "Don't worry. It's probably not really a ghost. It's just swamp gas." That would usually calm them down.

When I told the stories, I stuck pretty closely to the facts. Like *all* tour guides, I exaggerated a little bit here and there. These sorts of tricks are not exclusive to ghost tours—all tour guides do it. It doesn't make much of a difference with most crowds, since no one's taking notes or anything.

As a ghost investigator myself, an added bonus of the job was that I got to conduct mini investigations at a handful of hot spots a couple of times per week during the tours. These ten-to-fifteen minute stops could hardly be counted as scientific investigations—it was a group of tourists running around taking pictures. Sometimes we'd use more gear, like electromagnetic field readers, but a short stop doesn't really give you enough time to calibrate the things properly—not that anyone, on just about any investigation, ever uses those things correctly to begin with. No evidence you get on a ghost tour is ever going to be taken seriously as "evidence." But I've said it a hundred times—there's really no such thing as *good* ghost evidence, only "cool" ghost evidence.

We occasionally got some really cool stuff, too. In Death Alley, someone took a picture of me that showed an arm wearing a white sleeve outstretched in front of me—and no one present was wearing white sleeves. Just about a week later, someone took a picture that appeared to show a pant leg and shoe floating in midair—perhaps representing the leg of someone who fell to his death in the alley. You don't run into phantom pants in just *any* alley.

At the *Eastland* site, we would occasionally get faces in the waves, which, while easy to brush off as optical illusions, were pretty spooky. We also got so many orb shots there that we joked that the *Eastland* site was the place where all of the orbs in the city came to hang out.

And then there was Hull House.

Babies and B.S.

The last stop on most of my first tours, Hull House is a mansion just southwest of the Loop, the main downtown area in Chicago. Most of the ghost stories about it that go around are crap, and these days I'm loathe to take people there at all just because I feel like I'm encouraging some urban legends that really ought to die. No matter how much time I spend telling people that, no, contrary to what they may have heard, there is no "devil baby" buried in the garden next to the house, some people just don't get the message. The staff at the museum now operating in the house shouldn't have to deal with people showing up with shovels expecting to be allowed to dig up the garden looking for deformed corpses. I don't like feeling as though I'm giving the people at the museum the added headache of dealing with these people on top of their normal duties.

But in the first summer that I ran tours, we had more strange things happen there than at all the other stops on the tour combined.

Not too many years ago, I could have taken tour groups there, and it would have been the scariest stop on the tour for reasons that had nothing to do with ghosts—it was just a bad, bad neighborhood. A century ago, it was among the worst in the city—a distinction that stayed with the neighborhood until fairly recently. Crime, corruption, vice, sin, gambling, drugs, prostitution, and violence ran rampant—and that was just at the police station. The Maxwell Street Station, known as Bloody Maxwell, was known for coming up with creative ways of beating the living shit out of suspects to get them to confess to whatever they were accused of. The station itself is said to be haunted, not just by ghostly screams and wails, but by the smell of the trenches that ran through the cells to serve as bathrooms, garbage dumps, and drainage. Eew.

In 1888, a woman named Jane Addams came to town. She had been raised a very wealthy woman in western Illinois; her father was actually a friend of Abraham Lincoln. But after her father died, she and her friend Ellen moved to London and got work doing social services for the poor at Toynbee Hall, a settlement house. Before long, they decided that they could do the same work back in Chicago.

So they came back to town, found the worst neighborhood around, and were granted a rent-free lease on Hull

House, which was built by Mr. and Mrs. Charles Hull in 1856. Hull himself was known as one of the city's great eccentrics—he was known to have an interest in Spiritualism, which probably means that séances were held in the house around the time of the Civil War.

By 1889, when Charles Hull died, he still owned the house, but he had been living several blocks away in a somewhat nicer neighborhood—the South Halsted area had gone from being the middle of nowhere to being a neighborhood that even the more eccentric decent people avoided. The reading of Hull's will seems to be a scene right out of *Clue*. Several of his relatives gathered in the Ashland house, a simple row house that featured a large, heroic bust of Hull himself. Most of his nephews believed that he would be dividing his estate equally among them. But when the lawyer pulled the foolscap sheet from the envelope, it turned out that he'd left the whole of his estate to Helen Culver, his cousin and housekeeper. The nephews protested, but the will held, and Culver ended up granting Jane Addams a rent-free lease on the Halsted Street mansion.

When Addams moved in, the house was in between an Irish saloon and an undertaking parlor, which, given the kind of neighborhood it was, may have doubled as a saloon or brothel as well.

At Hull House, Addams set up a place where people could come to get an education, food, shelter, and health care. This was at a time when health care for women, even prenatal care, was practically unheard of in the neighborhood. This wasn't strictly due to the misogyny of the day; you have to remember that most of the women in the neighborhood were married to men who worked in low-down factories, slaughterhouses, and stockyards where they couldn't take a sick day—if they got sick, they'd just be fired. Therefore, if there was any money to be put toward health care at all (which would have been incredibly rare), it would inevitably go toward whomever in the family was working.

Soon there was hardly a person in Chicago who didn't know Addams's name, and everybody who was anybody came to visit her at Hull House. Daniel Burnham, one of the city's greatest architects, used to stop by regularly. So did Clarence Darrow, the greatest lawyer of the day—though his general tendency to smell like crap made him a bit unpopular there. This was not, mind you, a neighborhood where regular bathing was the norm to begin with. Darrow was a great lawyer, but he must have stunk to high heaven to offend anyone at Hull House.

Even before Addams moved in, though, the old mansion was rumored to be haunted. Addams described finding buckets of water kept on top of the staircase, which, she believed, was due to superstitions stating that ghosts could not cross water.[2]

Furthermore, Addams herself (who was not a believer in ghosts) reported hearing the sound of footsteps in Mrs.

2. This is actually a very old superstition about ghosts that was once very common. It's why Ichabod Crane has to get across the bridge to escape from the Headless Horseman.

Hull's old bedroom, which, thereafter, came to be referred to, at least jokingly, as "the Haunted Room."

Weirdest of all, perhaps, was the story of the devil baby. No one knows quite how it started, but in 1913, rumors went around that the devil had been born to a woman somewhere in the neighborhood. Explanations of exactly how this came about varied wildly, usually depending on the ethnicity of the woman telling the story, but one of the more common variations was that a woman had given birth to nine daughters, and, when she became pregnant again, her husband said, "I would rather have the next one be a devil than another girl!"

And, according to the story, he got his wish. The baby was born with red, scaly skin, hooves, a tail, a forked tongue, and a set of horns.[3]

The story continued that when the father brought the baby to Hull House, they passed a priest along the way, and the baby jumped up, grabbed the priest's cigar, and started to smoke it while cursing out the priest in English, Latin, and Italian. The baby, it was said, was fluent in a dozen languages and profane in all of them.

People tend to snicker at the story today, but, in those days, people really, really believed it. Hundreds of women

---

3. Interestingly, this sort of story is hardly unique to Hull House. In fact, it is almost exactly the same story as the one connected with the birth of the Jersey Devil, the creature that is said to stalk the Pine Barrens in New Jersey. Addams herself noted that, other than some variations of the story that involved a red automobile, the story could have been a thousand years old.

per day lined the steps to Hull House, demanding to see the devil baby.

Though initially furious about the whole thing, Addams (who insisted at length that no such child had ever been brought to the house) turned the women away. But she began to see the whole thing as an interesting sociological phenomenon. There were a lot of reasons that the women were so eager to believe the story—to some, it was a validation of the Old-World superstitions with which they had been raised in the Old Country that they had so recently left behind. Many, in fact, had no idea that their superstitions were local at all—people who had been raised to fear vampires had no idea that people in other parts of the world were raised any other way. For others, it was a rare chance to hold something over their husband's head. They wanted to see the child so that they could go home and say, "I have seen the devil baby. And if you don't start treating me nicer around here, that same thing could happen to us!"

Addams ended up using the whole experience as the basis for one of her books, *The Long Road of Woman's Memory*. Most people today believe Addams when she said that the story had absolutely no basis in fact, but the story still goes around. And, as superior to the people of a century ago as we can feel when we snicker at the story, there are still people who believe that there really was a devil baby—perhaps because certain unscrupulous ghost tour guides tell them there was. People still occasionally go to Hull House and bug the staff about it or claim to have photographed the devil baby's ghost.

Despite the fact that she was working against nearly unimaginable odds, Hull House was a success, and, after nearly half a century of running it, Addams became the first American woman to win a Nobel Peace Prize. When she died a few years later and her body was laid in state at Hull House, an estimated twenty thousand people per hour came to view the body.

By the time of Addams's death, the house had expanded enough to cover most of the block. In the 1960s, when the operations of the house were moved elsewhere, most of it had been torn down, leaving only the original house, which was restored as closely as possible to its original 1856 form, and the dining hall. The University of Illinois built its campus around it, and today it functions primarily as a museum.

But Hull House held on to its reputation as a haunted place. Not only is the house itself said to be haunted, but the garden next door, between the house and the present site of the dining hall, is sometimes called the Garden of Evil. It's not that there's an evil presence in there—it's just a good pun—but people who claim to be sensitive to ghosts tend to experience dizziness, shortness of breath, and things like that in there.

Rumors go around that the land upon which the house was built might at one time have been a graveyard for aborted fetuses (nonsense) or that, following the Fort

Dearborn Massacre, members of the Potawatomi tribe performed a Ghost Dance on the site to put a curse against the white man on it (also nonsense—or, if it *is* true, these must have been some pretty incompetent Ghost Dancers, seeing as how Addams won a Nobel Peace Prize for her work there). Other rumors suggest that it had once been an Indian burial ground, perhaps even the burial place of a Potawatomi shaman named Laughing Wolf. (Ken insists, from time to time, that this is actually true, but I have my doubts.) However, it probably *was* the site of the undertaking parlor that was on the grounds when Addams moved in. Or right nearby it anyway.

The house itself just *looks* like a haunted house—it's an old mansion with a creepy old staircase visible from the outside that curves up into the upper reaches of the house. The staircase was so well known for its creakiness that workers made sure it creaked when they restored it in the 1960s.

Even before I got the job, or moved to Chicago, I had heard of that staircase—one of the Chicago legends that had filtered through to the national ghost scene over the years was the story of "phantom monks"—ghosts that resembled guys in hooded gray robes—floating down the stairs. Monks are actually a fairly common type of apparition around Chicago—they're not really thought to be the ghosts of monks, as Hull House was never a monastery—the term "monks" is based only on the appearance. For several years, a photograph of monk ghosts on the Hull

House staircase had been floating around in ghost circles, though few people really get excited by it—the photo looks like little more than dark blobs around the stairs. But some insist that they can see the forms of guys in hooded robes—including a headless one—in these blobs.

Aside from the stories about Native American ghosts, Mrs. Hull, and the devil baby, no one is really sure who would be haunting the place now. However, it's easy to imagine that during, say, fever epidemics, an awful lot of people probably died there. Perhaps a couple of ghosts wandered over from the old undertaking parlor—there were plenty of ghost stories in the neighborhood a century ago.[4]

By the time the tour groups got there, the place was closed for the night, so Hector and I couldn't take people inside even if we wanted to, but from the front entryway we could see the old staircase through the window, and we could walk all around the grounds.

Strange things happened almost nightly.

Photographs of "monk ghosts" weren't exactly common, but they came up from time to time.

There was a cold spot in the garden that sort of came and went.

---

4. My favorite story concerns a ghost cited in the late nineteenth century in a house behind Hull House—where the University of Illinois Student Center is today. Apparently, one evening, during what must have been a very odd family reunion, a young man was shot in the face by his brother while in the process of trying to kill his mother. He stumbled out to the back porch before dying, and his ghost was seen sitting on a disused icebox on the porch so often that it became a regular spectacle in the neighborhood for a while.

Occasionally someone would take a photograph of the fountain in the garden, and the fountain wouldn't be present in the picture. We could see the sidewalk behind it that should have been bisected by the fountain, but not the actual fountain itself.

Camera malfunctions happened in the garden practically every night. One night, no one seemed to be able to take a picture of one particular tree. Pictures taken of it would show up blank, or cameras would suddenly run out of batteries or simply not function properly when someone tried to take a shot of it.

Younger kids would often get especially freaked out—many of them would look through the curtains into one particular window and say that they saw a woman in a white bonnet or a guy with an old-fashioned curly mustache. I was very careful not to mention either of these things ahead of time—and certainly some of the kids were just making stuff up—but the same stories came up over and over. If they had all been adults, I could say that maybe they had gotten together ahead of time, but the under-eight set is seldom that organized.

And photographs of strange things on the staircase happened every few nights.

It was here that I first really noticed that "haunted vibe." It wasn't there every night, but I got to a point where I could tell the second I stepped off the bus whether it was going to be an "active" night there.

Now, in my skepticism, I tried to explain all of this away. One of the main reasons Hull House is thought to be so haunted is that there are *lots* of ways to get false positives—perfectly ordinary photos that look ghostly—around there.

For instance, the smears on the window resulted in quite a few spooky-looking shots of the staircase. The combination of fingerprint smears and glare from the cameras created some fantastic ghost pictures, but they were just glare and smears.

There was a tendency for light from flashes to bounce off nearby buildings—there are lots of lights from nearby buildings reflecting lights onto the grounds—to result in orb pictures.

There are a couple of lamps inside of the house that, when photographed from the right angle, look a lot like feminine humanesque forms.

And though a lot of people felt uneasy in the garden, it's to be assumed that most of them felt that way because I'd just told them they would.

Most interesting of all to me were the monks on the staircase. Several people got shots of these and e-mailed them to me, and, while some of them were formed by a picture of light from the flash and the smears on the wall, the spookiest of them turned out to be the same thing over and over again: a reflection of the photographer's ear.

Of course, even if we could find a place that we absolutely *knew* had a specter in a white sheet banging around in the attic, it's a sure bet we'd get a lot of false positives there, too. When you're in a haunted house, you tend to blame ghosts for all of the noises you might otherwise blame—correctly—on the cat. Even in places that we think might really be haunted, we have to sort out the stuff we can't explain from the stuff that we can.

Most of the time, I kept my skepticism on the down-low during tours, partly because it made it more fun for me and partly because people would get so excited by pictures of smears that I didn't want to spoil it for them. One night, a couple created a regular sensation with a picture that appeared to show three hooded figures on a bench. I saw right away that it was a picture of the back of the guy's T-shirt, but kept my mouth shut. People were having too much fun, and I figured that once they got the thing onto their computer, the couple would see what the picture really was. There was no point in making them look silly in front of everyone.

But I sure couldn't explain everything that went on there. Especially in the early summer, when renovations began to take place at Hull House.

Now, ghost hunters don't agree on much. We all have our own theories and think everyone else is a kook. But one thing that is almost universally agreed upon is that when a place is undergoing construction or renovation, for one reason or another, the number of ghost sightings is likely to increase. No one can agree as to *why* this is, but it gets reported again and again.

One story that I often told was of the shutters for the top level of windows opening and closing. I had heard the story and repeated it, but had my doubts about it. Still, every tour, I would point to the shutters from the bus and ask everyone to make a note of whether they were opened or closed so we could see that they changed.

I remember fairly clearly the first night that the renovations began. Right off the bat, as we got off the bus, several people reported seeing some sort of weird, misty form inside of the place. Then, as a few of us walked across the porch toward the garden, we all heard, quite distinctly, the sound of a baby crying coming from the middle of the garden.

We walked around, looking to see if perhaps there was a cat in there making the sound, and we took picture after picture before we heard Hector shout, "Holy crap! The shutters!"

We ran back to the sidewalk, looked up, and saw that all of the upstairs shutters, which had been opened moments before, were closed.

For a few weeks thereafter, the shutters would change over the course of the time we were there, about two nights out of three.

Also around this time, we started getting a *bunch* of sightings of the ghost of a girl about twelve years old or so. There were a couple of very interesting pictures that seemed to show this ghost—even Willie's daughter got one. Willie claimed not to believe in ghosts, but insisted

"There's something in that house!" And, as skeptical as I was, I was starting to think so, too.

In fact, in all the tours I've given, I've only seen one photograph that I absolutely didn't think I could explain away. It was a photograph out in the garden, next to the fountain, that showed a big, orange blur. The blur looked, for all the world, like a shot of a young girl photographed from behind—you could clearly see the back of her head and the folds of something like a hoop skirt. I was standing right next to them when it was taken and saw it in the LCD screen, which meant that they hadn't just Photoshopped it in. We analyzed that shot like crazy and never came up with a very good explanation for it.

Pictures like that—and other strange things we couldn't explain—seemed to happen two nights out of three at that place all summer long. But while the place seemed actively haunted fairly regularly in the summer, it seemed quiet in the fall. I'm not sure if the ghosts quieted down or if I just learned enough about the environment of the place to be able to identify false positives more easily (and there are *lots* of ways to trick yourself or others into thinking that you're seeing a ghost there).

By winter, the site never seemed to be active at all anymore, other than the usual easy-to-explain orb shots and reflections of people's ears. Any night that it seemed active to people, it was only because we'd set up their minds to play tricks on them.

I also became increasingly upset about the effect that ghost tours and stories were having on Hull House itself, which is still an active organization. I hated to have customers e-mail me to angrily tell me that "those jerks" at Hull House wouldn't let them in to go ghost hunting when they showed up the next day.

The devil baby story is one example of something that really bugged me about the job—even though I encouraged people to be at least a little bit skeptical on tours, I was still encouraging a few urban legends that weren't entirely harmless, and, perhaps worse yet, I was sort of giving people permission to look for supernatural explanations whenever something strange happened. That's a dangerous thing to do.

As soon as I got to a point where I could vary the route, Hull House was one of the first places I stopped taking customers to. Hector and I still went there from time to time, just to check up on the place or dispel some of the myths customers had heard on other tours, but trips there became a lot less frequent.

Still, the things I'd seen there, more than any other place that first summer, made it harder and harder for me to brush off every strange thing as a trick of the imagination.

Through the Ages

You're always hearing things like "The ancient people of this region believed that ghosts were spirits condemned to live among the children of the animals they killed" or "The tribes here believed that the dead could return to be among the living on one night per year." Every time I hear people say something like this, I ask myself the same questions: Where did they get *that* idea? Who told them that? Did they really, truly believe it, or was it just a story that they told? It's not fair—how come *they* get to agree on what ghosts are and where they come from, and we don't?

As hunting for ghosts became more and more a part of my day, I came up with a lot of theories about ghosts and how to explain them—just *a lot* of them.

The most notable theory I hit on at the time was one that I hope will go down in history as Selzer's First Theorem: *Any* remotely spooky place that people sneak into in order to get wasted will eventually turn up on a TV *show, website, or book about ghosts.* Spookiness + drunkenness is a regular formula for ghost sightings. Ghost hunting is really not the sort of thing you ought to do while drunk, but, when we would make a pub stop on some of the tours, I would tell people that the two sorts of people who see ghosts most often are children under about the age of five and older people who've been drinking heavily—if they had a drink at the pub, they'd probably greatly increase their chances of seeing a ghost.

While we were at the pub, I had a chance to chat with the customers. Here, people would tell me their own ghost stories. As much as I enjoyed hearing them, I quickly realized that all ghost stories are pretty much the same. I heard a few of the same things over and over and over again.

These included:

1. "My son said he saw his grandfather, whom he had never met, in his room. An hour later, we got a call that his grandfather had died."

I hear variations of this story almost as often as I hear from people who say that their grandparents hung around with Al Capone. Of the two, the ghost stories are frankly the ones I'm more likely to believe.

Stories of kids seeing a dead grandparent, either on the night of the person's death or for months after it, are really quite common. Many people told me that they'd seen their toddler playing with someone and clearly having a conversation with the person when there was no one there.

The kid would later describe their playmate as matching a description of some long-deceased ancestor. Often, the kid would even have information that he or she could only have heard from that ancestor. These stories tested my skepticism the most; they're common enough that I couldn't simply brush them off as imagination every time, and most of the scientific theories I hit on over the years didn't come close to explaining them.

2. "We think our house is built on an Indian burial ground."

Normally, this strikes me as the sort of thing that they should have noticed when they dug out the basement. However, it's certainly not impossible—or even all that uncommon—to find houses in the Chicago area that are built over graves, Indian and otherwise, that may be buried so deep beneath landfills that the basement just didn't go down far enough to get to the bodies.

3. "My grandfather's clock stopped the day he died."

This sort of story is rather well known; in the nineteenth century, it was even the basis of "My Grandfather's Clock," a tremendously popular parlor song by Chicagoan Henry Clay Work, who was responsible for some of the most maudlin parlor songs of the Victorian era. (Which is really saying something. The song about the clock that "stopped short, never to go again, when the old man died" after "ninety years without slumbering ... his life seconds numbering" was actually one of Work's cheerier numbers—look up his other big hit, "Come Home, Father," if you *really* want a good time.) Variations of this—mechanical or electrical disturbances at the moment of someone's death—are common stories.

4. "**We set up a digital voice recorder and recorded a voice saying, 'Get out!'**"

There must be some kind of memo going around in the spirit world saying, "When those guys with the microphones show up, tell 'em to get out!" Phrases like "Leave" and "We don't want you here!" are also common.

The practice of using audio recorders to look for ghostly voices that can't be heard with the naked ear is known as EVP (electronic voice phenomenon), and eventually it became my job on ghost hunts. As the EVP guy in the group, I've never run across a voice telling me to get out, but the first ghost who tells me something like that is getting a real tongue-lashing from me. "I'll get out when I damn well please!" I'll say. "You're the one who's dead around here! Don't make me get out my proton pack! We can cross the streams with the 2.0 models, you know!"

Speaking hypothetically, if there are ghosts in the world, I respect their right to exist, but I don't have much patience for those who think they can push the living around.

The closest thing I've seen to this, honestly, was one night at the Congress Hotel, where letters in a sealed message board had been arranged to spell out "U Will Die." The security guards swore they hadn't done it. It still seems like a pretty obvious prank to me, but if it was a ghost, this ghost must have learned all its tricks from B-grade horror movies. How is "U Will Die" a prediction, anyway? Of course we're going to die! I'd have been more impressed if it provided a specific name and date.

5. "My grandmother always smelled of cigarettes and lilac perfume. She's been dead for years, but we still smell that particular scent around the house sometimes."

"Olfactory apparitions" are actually very common—and we tend to take them a bit more seriously than other sightings, since smell is the sense least likely to be hallucinated.

Almost every story I heard fell into one of these categories.

Ghost stories have probably been going around since the beginning of storytelling, and people have been debating whether ghosts have existed for centuries. The Chinese philosopher Mo Tzu was arguing in favor of the idea that they existed in the fifth century BCE. The ancient Greeks had stories about them. And even then, most of the ghost stories people told were pretty much the same as the ones they tell now. Most of them, then as now, follow one of two basic formulas: someone dies, then returns, or the protagonist of a story meets a person who turns out to be dead.

Most ghost stories now are still variations on these themes, though they've changed with the times. For instance, stories of vanishing hitchhikers like Resurrection Mary have changed as modes of transportation have changed, but the basic story of a disappearing traveler goes back centuries—there's even a variation, of sorts, on it in the New Testament (Acts 8:26–39), in which the Apostle Philip vanishes after baptizing a eunuch in whose chariot he's been hitching a ride. Now, of course, hitchhikers vanish out of cars, not chariots.

Ghost stories in America were always common. Most of the earliest European settlers tended to blame weird things they saw or heard on the Devil, not ghosts, but, if one reads Washington Irving's "The Legend of Sleepy Hollow," it's pretty clear that small villages were full of local ghost stories by the end of the eighteenth century and that many of these stories were already regarded as ancient.

One of the first ghosts to be widely publicized in America was the ghost of Nelly Butler, who was first reported to appear in Maine in 1799. According to the stories about her, she started out as a regular old poltergeist, throwing things around the room and beating on walls. Then, around 1800, she began to talk. Eventually, she even began to appear as a floating humanesque form who would engage people in conversation—often long conversations about religion (a lot of nineteenth-century ghosts seemed to be very much in the habit of giving lengthy lectures on religion).

A fellow named Reverend Abraham Cummings arrived on the scene ready to debunk the whole thing, then came away a believer. He built his career as a preacher recounting the story of Nelly and her religious chats, holding it up as solid proof of the afterlife. Many people agreed that it was incontestable proof. In fact, though, Reverend Cummings seems to have made the whole thing up—Nelly wasn't a real ghost at all, but a literary device that he used in sermons and insisted was a true story (which was not very preacherly of him, if you ask me). Still, the fact that people bought it indicates that belief in ghosts was very much alive at the time.

One of the first "real" ghosts in America to become famous was the Bell Witch, a malevolent ghost who stalked the Bell family of Adams, Tennessee, beginning in 1817. The story of the Bell Witch remains one of the strangest and most exciting ghost stories ever told.

The story begins with John Bell encountering a bizarre animal, having the body of a dog and the head of a rabbit, on his property. It fled when he shot at it. Shortly thereafter, the family began hearing strange noises around the property. Bell's youngest daughter, Betsy, began to feel as though she were being poked, prodded, and assaulted by a strange, unseen force. Soon, the family began to report a voice that sounded like a whispering old woman crying or singing hymns.

The assaults on Betsy began to get worse—she would report getting her hair pulled and her face slapped hard enough to leave marks on her face.[5]

Eventually, the family had a neighbor, James Johnston, spend a night at the house. Johnston reported feeling his face slapped and feeling the bedcovers ripped off of his bed, prompting him to get up and shout, "Who are you, and what do you want?"

Johnston was clearly ahead of his time, using that line more than a century before it would become one of the biggest cliché lines of horror movies. It worked better for him than it usually does in the movies—the disturbances stopped.

But they were back the next night, and they became even more vicious. The fame of the ghost spread, and people came to see things for themselves. Even Andrew Jackson, the general who would later become president, and his men reportedly spent a night on the property challenging the "witch" to a fight and got their asses kicked so thoroughly that Jackson said he'd rather face the entire British army alone than fight the Bell Witch again.

Over time, the voice got louder, and the "witch," who came to be known as Kate, began to shout at people, order them around, and, like any good nineteenth-century

5. One theory popularized by television movies is that the "witch" was the result of mental anguish within Betsy caused by her father sexually abusing her, but there's absolutely no evidence that John Bell was an abusive father. There's no proof that he *wasn't*, but I feel like I ought to mention this, since so many people seem to accept the theory as fact.

ghost, lecture them on religion at great length. When Betsy decided to marry a boy named Joshua Gardner, the witch ordered her not to and tormented her endlessly until she broke off the engagement. It even took credit for killing John Bell when he died, reportedly laughing and shouting, "I've got him this time! He'll never get up from that bed again!" The witch, it seems, had replaced his usual tonic with some sort of mysterious poison.

Troy Taylor, the guy who signed my checks at Chicago Spooks, happened to be one of the world's greatest experts on the case. He theorized that the ghost was some sort of spirit that had been appearing in various guises for centuries and had been disturbed when the Bell family accidentally dug up a grave near a cave on the property.[6] Others (and Troy may want to kick my ass for siding with them) point to the fact that a great deal of the story as we know it comes from a "family history" written decades after the fact by Richard Bell, who was only a little kid when the whole thing happened. It's generally agreed that there was some legitimate poltergeist activity going on, but Richard had a good thirty years to embellish the story in his mind and around the campfire. His version is the primary source of most of the best parts of the story. His account, for instance, is the only evidence we have that Andrew Jackson had ever even heard of the Bell Witch.

---

6. Today, the Bell Witch Cave is something of a tourist attraction. Troy takes groups out there from time to time.

As the nineteenth century progressed and cameras were invented, people almost immediately hit on the idea of trying to use the newfangled contraptions to capture images of ghosts. Unfortunately, people also hit on the idea of using them to *fake* ghost pictures right away, and some people made a lot of money taking pictures of people and claiming that the pictures showed ghosts in the background. Practically no ghost photo from the early days is ever held up as genuine ghost evidence today.

Organized, semi-scientific ghost hunting really didn't take off as a popular pastime until the nineteenth century, when the Spiritualist movement—the movement based around the belief that, instead of going to heaven, dead people turned into spirits that floated around and could be communicated with by "mediums"—was all the rage.

The Spiritualist movement began in 1848 when a family by the name of Fox rented a house in Hydesville, New York. Leah, Margaretta, and Kate Fox, the daughters of the family, began to hear lots of odd knocking sounds around the house, which they began to attribute to a ghost named "Mr. Splitfoot," which was a colloquial name for Satan.

Why exactly the girls just went straight to thinking that Satan had nothing better to do with his time than bang around on their walls, instead of blaming the sound on, say, a raccoon, is up to some debate, but the girls claimed to be able to communicate with whatever the thing was. Kate called out, "Here, Mr. Splitfoot. Do as I do!" and began to clap her hands. The ghost clapped along.

Soon, they had worked out a system of communication where the ghost—which they apparently no longer thought was the devil—would answer questions with two knocks on the wall meaning yes and silence meaning no.

Eventually, they ended up with a story that the entity was the ghost of a man who had been murdered on the property. Hundreds of people came to the house to see demonstrations of the Fox sisters in action, and eventually P. T. Barnum had them doing their "act" in New York. They became among the first people to make a career for themselves as "mediums."

This was the beginning of an entire movement. The idea that spirits of the dead were not yet in heaven, but at some place in between, floating around knocking on tables, became a whole new religion. Throughout the late nineteenth century, there were countless self-styled mediums offering to communicate with the dead for a fee.

These "mediums" came up with all sorts of ways to talk to the dead. In addition to having the "spirits" knock on tables, some dabbled in "automatic writing," and others spread the popularity of séances in which participants would sit around a table trying to get ghosts to ring a bell or knock on the wall. Really accomplished mediums could even get "ectoplasm," a misty, sheetlike material said to be physical evidence of the spirit, to float around the room.

It was the popularity of these séances that led to the first scientific investigations of ghosts. Even believers knew that there were a lot of frauds out there, and debunkers, eventually including such luminaries as Sir Arthur Conan Doyle and Harry Houdini, set out not to debunk the whole idea of Spiritualism, but to separate the real mediums from the frauds. Even the movement's most ardent supporters admitted that most of the mediums out there were full of shit—knocks on the walls were hardly difficult to fake, after all.

Most of the phenomenon, in fact, was ridiculously easy to fake. In 1888, the Fox sisters confessed that they had produced the knocking sounds by cracking their toes (though they took it back a year later). The "ectoplasm" some mediums produced was pretty generally cheesecloth that they had rolled up and hidden in some of their more nefarious bodily orifices—at least one debunker noted that you could tell where the cheesecloth had been hidden by the way it smelled. Others, it seems, learned to swallow and regurgitate the stuff.

Spiritualism and séances remained popular with people of all social classes throughout the nineteenth century and on through the first half of the twentieth century. They experienced major revivals every time there was a particularly bloody war that made people want to communicate with recently departed soldiers (the Civil War and World War I eras were boom times). While the Spiritualist religion has mostly died out since then, the séances and practices it popularized, such as sitting around tables waiting for them to vibrate or waiting for knocking sounds to appear, are still very much alive today. The difference is that séances of the nineteenth century were novelties—no one, except for some of the more devoutly religious types, seemed ashamed to give it a try. Today, it's more often looked upon as something for teenage girls to do at slumber parties or for flaky people to demonstrate on cable TV.

As people began to debunk phony mediums, others began to look into haunted places to see if ghosts and spirits could be scientifically proven or disproven or if anyone besides mediums could see them. Various groups formed with the intent of either proving or disproving ghosts and Spiritualism. Most of them died out rapidly; those that survived tended to be those who were a mix of skeptics and believers. The best known was probably the English Society of Psychical Research, which formed in 1882 with the intent of "examining allegedly psychic phenomenon in a scientific and unbiased way." Members eventually included Sigmund Freud, Carl Jung, Sir Arthur Conan Doyle, and a whole host of famous (as these things go) physicists and philosophers. They (the society, not the people) still exist today.

In the early twentieth century, they became best known for their member Harry Price. Price grew up fascinated by stage magic and, after marrying into money and finding that he didn't need to get a *real* job, became a ghost hunter.

While he was certainly no scientist himself, Price's experience in stage magic made him a natural at exposing the tricks of fake mediums. He spent years putting supposed psychics to the test, using methods of his own devising. But it was with his investigations of Borley Rectory, which he called "The Most Haunted House in England," that he brought ghost hunting into the scientific age.

If I bought an old house with a name like Borley Rectory, I'd be pretty disappointed if it *wasn't* haunted. The house itself was built in 1862 near Borley Church, a little church next to a graveyard that dated to the twelfth century. One of the more venerable of the many "ghost of a disgraced nun" stories that go around holds that there was once a fourteenth-century monastery on the Borley Rectory grounds,[7] in which a nun was bricked into a wall alive within the convent as punishment for her affair with a monk.

The story appears to have no basis in fact, but, of course, it's one of those things that the fourteenth-century monks probably wouldn't have gone out of their way to leave proof of, so there's no way to know for sure.

When Borley Rectory was built, ghostly footsteps began to be heard almost immediately. Around 1900, the ghostly apparition of a nun was seen on the grounds. Other people reported seeing a ghostly coach driven by headless drivers. The owner at the time—Reverend Henry Bull—seems to have thought all of this was pretty nifty. He and his son, who later took over the house, spent many evenings sitting around waiting for the ghostly nun to show up.

Things really heated up at the rectory in the 1920s, when new occupants found a human skull on the prop-

---

7. Though not exclusively British, the "former monastery" stories are sort of the English equivalent of the American "Indian burial ground" stories.

erty. They began to report all sorts of weird stuff, like bells ringing and mysterious footsteps. They sold the house after a short time, possibly due more to its bad condition than any hauntings.

By this time, over a dozen people had seen the ghostly nun. A handful had seen the carriage, and a couple had seen a headless man walking around—Borley Rectory was apparently *the* place to hang out if you were a headless ghost. It was around this time that Harry Price was brought in by a newspaper to begin investigating the place.

In the late 1930s, Price recruited about four dozen volunteers to keep constant patrol on the house, using such basic equipment as cameras, string, tape measures, and watches with second hands. He issued a pamphlet to them instructing them in the proper way to investigate the house, making this investigation perhaps the first truly organized modern ghost hunt.

The investigation went on for a couple of years, with investigators experimenting with different kinds of equipment and holding séances. Information from these séances indicated that the nun was the ghost of a woman who had been murdered on the grounds in the 1660s.

Borley Rectory burned to the ground in 1939. Price did some quick digging in the rubble and found a St. Ignatius medal and a couple of bones that were said to be the remains of the nun. Some said that they were actually the bones of a pig, but they were reburied before anyone could find out for sure.

Price ended up publishing two books on the strange phenomena associated with the house, which some members of the Society for Psychical Research held up as proof of the existence of ghosts and the afterlife. After Price's death in 1947, however, attacks came from all sides—a report issued by the Society itself determined that most of the things reported in the house were natural phenomena, such as rats, and that others had been hoaxes. Many believed that Price himself had been behind many of the hoaxes.

Today, many still believe that the rectory was genuinely haunted, though most feel that Price was more of a showman than anything else and that his works should be viewed with skepticism. Some point out that he mainly reported what people said they experienced and how they reacted—he never said that he was behind the experiences they were having, but he didn't exactly say that he wasn't, either.

When I went back and read all of this in the early days of my quest to get to the bottom of this whole ghost business, most of it was familiar to me from my days as a preteen strange-phenomena buff. I especially enjoyed reading that Harry Price had investigated "Gef the Talking Mongoose," a poltergeist-type talking ghost that claimed to be a talking mongoose. I remembered reading about Gef when I was in fourth grade (and, in what was at the time a rare show of skepticism, thinking it sounded ridiculous).

Reading about all of this stuff in more detail—in an age when I could go online and see a skeptical response that was sorely lacking from ghost books and TV shows when I was a kid—didn't do too much to alleviate my skepticism. I still felt, though, that many skeptics were being too quick to brush things off. The fact that some of the evidence at Borley Rectory was faked or simply misinterpreted natural phenomena doesn't mean that the place wasn't haunted; it just means that people sometimes played tricks and made mistakes there. With forty-eight volunteers working on the place, it's inevitable that some of them are going to get bored and play a joke now and then.

Even if some of the phenomena was genuinely ghostly, in any given house that's thought to be haunted, it's natural to blame ghosts for noises that you would otherwise blame on the cat. But because you blame the ghost for one noise that the cat made doesn't mean that the ghost isn't around.

Let's stroke my vanity a bit and call this Selzer's Second Theorem: *The more haunted a place is, the more false positives will be reported, even if the haunting is genuine.*

If I may be a bit crude, I'll nickname this the Fart Theory. Reporting a ghost can be about like reporting a fart. Say you have a roommate who really cuts one on the day he moves in—a big noisy one that makes you think he must have just eaten a big bowl of sulphur and washed it down with onion juice. Over the first couple of days he lives with you, you find that these emissions come out of his butt pretty regularly. Thereafter, when you hear a shoe squeak or when a garbage truck rolls by outside, you'll assume that the roommate farted again. You'll be wrong, but that doesn't mean he didn't do it the first time, and it doesn't mean he won't do it again, no matter how often he denies it or tries to blame it on the nearest dog.

The same is true of ghosts—once a ghost is seen in a house, people will blame every stray noise and shadow on it. It stands to reason that the more haunted a place actually is, the more false positives will be reported. No matter how many sightings get explained away, it doesn't mean that a place isn't haunted to begin with.

But it's also difficult not to notice that all of the ghost hunting of the last century has failed to turn up anything conclusive. If ghosts are conscious entities, floating around with thoughts and agendas of their own, and possessing any means to communicate, they sure as hell must not want anyone to know about it.

On the other hand, what about all of the firsthand accounts that one hears of hauntings and phenomena that can only be classified as supernatural?

For instance, my great-grandma Eloise wrote about an experience her father, my great-great-grandpa Harry, had one day. He was a skeptic himself—he would chuckle whenever people talked about séances or ghosts—but one wintry day he was stoking the fire in a stove in a soda fountain that he ran when he dropped the coal bucket and walked over to his wife, saying, "I have just seen a young man in uniform fall in a battle!" Skeptical though he was, he took note of the date. A few weeks later, word came that on that day, his nephew, Delmar, had been killed in France, where he was fighting in World War I.

This is similar to so many of the stories I heard during breaks in the tour. People claimed that, along with other witnesses, they had seen recently departed friends walking down the road or that their young children reported encounters with people who turned out to fit the description of a long-dead previous owner of their house, including information that the kids couldn't have possibly known but turned out to be accurate.

To believe all of these people, I'd have to be a little bit gullible. But in order to believe that *all* of them were lying to me, I'd have to be a total dick.

There are some things that can't simply be brushed off.

The Science of the Supernatural

Mathematics prove that there are more than three dimensions in the world, but our brains aren't sophisticated enough to perceive them. I, for one, can't even conceive of how a fourth or fifth dimension is supposed to look. I'm not sure anyone can.

Okay. To be honest, I don't know if all that stuff about mathematics proving the existence of extra dimensions is true. The scientist I heard that from isn't a real scientist at all—he was just a character in an issue of *The Amazing Spider-man*. And he turned out to be a bad guy, so his word is probably even less reliable.

It sounds about right to me, but once math and science get into those theoretical realms of imaginary numbers, algorithms and stuff, I tend to get lost. My brain just can't get wrapped around that sort of thing. If there's a fourth dimension (and I know that most *Twilight Zone* episodes opened with Rod Serling saying, "There is a fifth dimension," which I suppose implies there must be a fourth one out there), I'll go ahead and assume that I can't perceive it.

One thing I do know is that different brains work in different ways. Some people can look at a math problem and see something that makes sense. Others can look at a poem and understand it on levels that some of those mathematicians are never going to see. Others understand fashion, cars, or wine. Some people actually claim to understand what's fun about hanging out in trendy nightclubs.

The fact that I'm not much of a scientist, though, doesn't mean that I can't understand the basics of the scientific method and approach ghosts critically. But the sheer fact that I hang out with a crowd of ghost hunters is going to make a lot of skeptics hesitant, at the very least, to count me among their number. Skeptics and people who believe in ghosts tend not to get along.

To many skeptics, people who believe in ghosts are gullible, superstitious flakes. Many ghost buffs, in turn, think that skeptics are a bunch of know-it-all jerks who are out to spoil their fun and just don't understand that there's anything in the world that hasn't been explained already. I've had plenty of people step on the bus and say, "Boy, I hope there aren't any skeptics on this tour."

There's a reason for this sentiment—some ghost fans *are* gullible, superstitious flakes who believe any stupid thing they see on the Internet. And a lot of skeptics *are* loud-mouthed jerks who try to win the argument against believers talk-radio style: by shouting louder than everyone else and insisting that anyone who doesn't think science has already explained everything is a moron. Both sides can be equally dogmatic.

But while there are always debates between skeptics and believers, people who believe in ghosts (and other weird stuff) spend most of their time arguing with each other.

There are a few basic things ghost hunters can agree on—for instance, places that are thought to be haunted tend to exhibit a lot of little environmental oddities, such as cold spots, weird electrical stuff, a tendency for batteries to drain very quickly, and so on. But the question becomes: are these environmental oddities there because the place is haunted, or are these environmental oddities just making us *think* the place is haunted? Some skeptics will immediately say it's always, always just your mind playing tricks on you, nothing more. And some ghost fans are ready to punch anyone who suggests that the tapping noise they hear on the window might be a tree, not a dead person.

I usually side with the skeptics and scientists. But I also know that there's plenty that we don't know about the world yet. Skeptics will claim that ghosts, if they're present, should have a measurable impact on the environment, but who's to say if we've invented the right instruments to measure them yet? The scientific method holds that if something is real, it should be verifiable by scientific experiments that can be performed by anyone, even a child, and that will bring about the same results over and over. This is true, but it leaves out the fact that some of these experiments can only be performed by a child if that child happens to know how to operate a particle accelerator.

But the scientists are pretty much right—almost every ghost report can be explained away as something other than a dead guy. There are lots of normal things in the environment that can make you *think* there's a ghost around.

For one thing, there's infrasound—low-frequency noises caused by objects vibrating at a rate of about 18 hertz. That's about the speed at which your eyeballs vibrate (which, as I understand it, they do all the time). Some scientific studies, particularly those by Vic Tandy, a lecturer at Coventry University in England, have indicated that the presence of these sounds—which can't be heard by the human ear—in an environment can have a weird psychological effect on people. It can make the hair on the back of your neck stand up, and it can give you a distinct sensation that someone, or thing, is in the room with you. In fact, during hyperventilation, your vibrating eyeballs can not only make you think you're seeing a vague gray form, but they can also produce the very infrasound that makes you think that the gray form is a ghost.

Infrasounds can even occasionally cause lightweight objects to move—they may be the culprit when the curtains flutter in a room. Since old pipe organ pipes are loaded (as I understand it) with infrasound, this may explain why so many old churches and theaters are said to be haunted (and practically all of them are).

Then there's carbon monoxide. Carbon monoxide poisoning can cause dread, dementia, and hallucinations—extreme cases have people hearing the sound of bells or footsteps and even seeing apparitions up and walking around. This was first identified as the source of reports of a haunted house in the 1920s. However, it's unlikely that this can be used to explain too many ghost reports, because when the poisoning gets bad enough to cause such hallucinations, the sufferer will probably be dead before he or she can report them to the local ghost hunters.

And these are just a couple of the more interesting ways we skeptics explain things away. There are also dozens upon dozens of regular scientific explanations—drug-fueled hallucinations, the wind blowing over pipes, seismic activity, and just plain tricks of the mind and imagination.

But these don't explain everything away. They certainly didn't explain all of the stories I heard from people on the bus, and they didn't explain some of what I was seeing on my first investigations.

I kept an open mind during tours and investigations, of course, but I also had a little voice in the back of my head during every ghost hunt saying, "Hey, stupid! There's no such thing as ghosts!" I would respond by saying, "Shut up, brain—this beats bagging groceries!"

Finally that voice in my head got more reasonable. "Fine," it said. "Go looking for ghosts. But at least talk to all of your scientist buddies to see if there might, conceivably, be anything to all of this ghost business. Some scientific way that an apparition could haunt these old buildings and alleys."

That was fair enough. After all, the idea that ghosts are a genuine scientific phenomenon, not a supernatural one, has been going around for a long time. Not everyone who believes in ghosts believes that these ghosts are transparent spirits that fly out of the body at the moment of death.

I began talking to every scientist I knew and every scientist I could track down in an attempt to see if there might be some way to use science to explain ghosts rather than just using it to brush them off, but with every physics discussion I got into, I realized I was in over my head. I felt like a four-year-old getting a lesson in algebra. Even back when I was in a high school classroom full of kids who believed that Adam and Eve had a pet dinosaur, I was a pretty average science student. I suppose I can claim to know the basics of science pretty well, but once people start trying to explain physics to me, I start to feel like a blubbering idiot. I tend, for better or worse, simply to take scientists at their word.

And when I started asking the scientists that I knew if ghosts exist, most simply said no outright. But this wasn't very scientific of them at all. The term "ghost" has enough meanings that it can be considered a variable. Even I, a non-scientist who holds out hope of one day owning a real lightsaber and, if I can afford it, a space ship, knew that they shouldn't be passing judgment on a variable before its parameters were defined.

It's partly the fault of the flakier ghost fans that the scientists were jumping to conclusions so fast, but another part of the reason that so many say no right away is that scientists are just as cliquish as those of any other profession. If they said yes, or even maybe, they'd get picked on by some of their colleagues.

Finally, I found one scientist who was willing to talk about ghosts with me. Seth Kleinschrodt, my old partner in crime from Des Moines, had grown up to be an engineer. When I got ahold of him, he was teaching classes on science at the University of Iowa, and he had kept up his interest in ghosts. In particular, he was interested in how they could be explained scientifically. Just the sort of thing I wanted to talk about. And when I asked him to explain it to me the way he'd explain it to a four-year-old, he was able to do it.

"When a person dies traumatically," he explained, "it's very much an electrical process. A big jolt of energy. And when you get into upper-level physics, it's all about how a jolt of energy will leave an impact on the environment basically forever." He hoped one day to prove that a sudden, traumatic death could, in theory, create an "apparition."

He theorized that one could actually re-create the effect and create an actual ghost, if one had a particle accelerator and someone willing to die traumatically in front of it or something like that. He did manage to go over my head eventually. But the general idea was actually one of the most common things you hear among people trying to reconcile a belief in ghosts with a belief in science: ghosts aren't "souls," they're energy. One of the most basic scientific laws that we all remember from school is that matter and energy—including mental energy—can neither be created nor destroyed, only transferred and transformed.

To put it another way, most of the attempts to explain ghosts with science can be simplified by describing the concept of "bad vibes." Everyone has had the experience of walking into a place and just getting a bad feeling about the joint. There's just a chance that this bad feeling may have come from the residual energy left behind by people who saw or experienced something unpleasant in the place sometime before. Ghosts, in theory, are sort of a more extreme, concentrated version of these vibes.

In fact, I talked about this concept of ghosts all the time on the tours—the term people like to use for this is "psychic imprint." Or, if that's too New Agey for you, "residual haunting." One example we often gave was a psychic imprint supposedly left behind by Highball, a dog who was present at the St. Valentine's Day Massacre.

Though he wasn't shot at, Highball was apparently so freaked out that he left behind an "imprint," or some sort of freaked-out vibe. Dogs tended to go nuts when they walked by the site of the massacre up until about the 1990s, when the imprint apparently dissipated into the environment. The ghosts-as-science theorists pretty generally agree that these energies, whatever they are, don't last forever. You almost never hear about ghosts of people who died more than about three hundred years before; there are ghosts reported on the sites of plenty of Civil War battlefields, but you seldom hear about ghosts on the sites of battles from, say, the Hundred Years' War.

The idea that ghosts are "caused" by a sudden jolt of some form of mental energy or another isn't a new one, either. Variations on the idea have been going around for well over a century.

In 1907, Dr. Bernard Hollander addressed a group of scientists at the Lyceum Club in London and reported that ghosts were no longer the stuff of superstition—they were scientific fact. The speech was reported in great detail in the *Chicago Tribune*.

Ghosts were the result, he said, of "the wireless telegraph of the mind." They were not souls, but "living thoughts projected into space by the personality at the death moment."[8]

The human brain, he explained, was a storehouse of energy. He believed that the energy was electrical in nature, but admitted that this was sort of an open question. The bottom line, though, was that a thought in the brain was a

---

8. "How to See Ghosts," *Chicago Tribune*, June 2, 1907.

physical thing. A "mental picture" was a construction of images and energies within the brain. Some people, such as great leaders, were apt to send out these mental images into the ether. These images produced in the brain may be sent out to sensitive people who may, in fact, receive the images in the form of a vague presentiment if they happen to be in the right state of mind. This explanation, he claimed, was "the simplest explanation of telepathy, and removes it at once from the realm of the supernatural."

Hollander explained that ghosts were a form of this sort of telepathy, and he cited the "familiar example" of a murdered man being seen in ghostly form at the scene of the crime. At the moment of murder, the mysterious energies of his mind would be wrought to such a fever pitch that they would become reality, forming a sort of picture of the man's image or personality that may attach itself to the area. Certain people might pick it up visually under certain circumstances. Others never will, even though it's always there, waiting to be seen, because their brains just aren't set up for it.

The specter, Hollander went on, may be a perfect image or one that is vague and undefined, depending on the exact nature of the mental energies exerted. It may stay in one place or rove around. It may stay only a short time before fading away, or it may linger for generations. It may not be seen often, but certain people with their brains wired in a certain way may notice it when they're in exactly the right frame of mind. This, he explained, was why ghosts may be seen only infrequently. "This will explain," he said, "why daring men who come [to haunted houses] with pistols and swords[9] will not see a ghost at first. So long as they are wide awake and belligerent, their brain is too active to receive the image. It is only when they get tired that the impression is made upon their brains."[10]

Dr. Hollander was a fairly well-regarded scientist in his day, and many who attended his lecture seem to have received this information as cold, solid fact. How much of it stands up today is another matter—Dr. Hollander is best known today for his interest in phrenology, the practice of figuring out people's mental capacity and character by measuring their skulls. No less an authority than Mr. Smithers on *The Simpsons* said that phrenology "was dismissed as quackery 160 years ago." After all, if we can send out thoughts over a sort of wireless telegraph of the mind, why can't we get it to work under laboratory conditions? Why hasn't the military found a way to transmit data via brain waves? In short, why haven't we made any real progress in learning to control or understand this stuff?

Still, his theory is as close as anyone has come to summing up how ghosts come to exist if they're not souls floating out of the body at death. Many of the scientists I discussed this with admitted that, while Dr. Hollander was

---

9. Judging from newspaper reports of the day, swords and pistols were actually much more common ghost-hunting tools than you'd think. One *Chicago Tribune* article from the late nineteenth century ("The Ghost of Lincoln Street," February 17, 1888) even spoke of a ghost that was appearing nightly, drawing large crowds to come and shoot at it.

10. "How to See Ghosts," *Chicago Tribune*, June 2, 1907.

probably incorrect about the precise mechanics of the process, he may have been on to something.

I wouldn't say I *believe* that some form of concentrated mental energy can create a "living thought" that can be seen as a ghost, but I *suspect* that something like that might happen under certain circumstances. If there's one thing I learned from my investigations into ghosts as science, it's that there's a difference between believing and suspecting.

Of course, what, exactly, this "concentrated mental energy" is, how it is generated, how it impacts the environment, and whether it even exists in the first place are still lingering questions. They may never be answered—though plenty of people have tried.

In the 1970s, when there was a lot of scientific research into psychic phenomena going on, a researcher in Toronto headed up what became known as the Philip Experiment.

At the time, a lot of research was going into poltergeists—ghosts that aren't really *seen*, but will manifest by throwing things around, tugging at your clothes, etc.—and the research suggested that the phenomena might not be of ghostly origin at all. A large number of poltergeists seemed to be reported in houses in which there was a young teenage girl. The idea that many scientists came up with during the late 1960s was that these disturbances that were blamed on ghosts were actually the result of telekinetic energy. In other words, it wasn't a dead person, it was the pent-up mental energy of the living girl that was causing all of the dishes to fly around the room.[11]

Intrigued by the notion that a ghost could be "created" by living people, a fellow named Dr. A. R. G. Owen gathered a group of people to see if the effect could be recreated. To begin with, they constructed an elaborate biography of a fictional man named Philip Aylseford. According to the story, Philip was born in 1624, was knighted at age sixteen, got married, worked as a secret agent, and fell in love with a gypsy girl. When his wife learned of the affair, she had the gypsy burned at the stake as a witch, and Philip, distraught, committed suicide in 1654. With a story like that, it would be a shame if there *wasn't* a ghost.

In 1972 (this certainly sounds like something that would have happened in the 1970s, doesn't it?), the group began to meditate, visualize, and talk about the details of Philip's life, trying to teach themselves to "believe" in him. They conducted nineteenth-century-style séances, sitting around a table and attempting to get Philip to communicate with them by banging on the table or making it levitate.

Early results, as you can probably imagine, were pretty much inconclusive. Some members of the group began to report that they felt as though there was a presence in the room, but that was about it. Then, amazingly, "Philip" began

---

11. It seems a bit odd that this would be taken seriously as a scientific explanation, but it often has been. Others have, of course, been skeptical about this. The classic catch phrase for skeptics here is "If there's anyone here who can move objects with their mind, will you please raise my hand?" I've asked it on the tour myself; the first time some kid manages to raise my hand, I'm taking that kid straight to Vegas.

to communicate, answering yes-or-no questions by tapping on the table.

The group engaged "Philip" in several long question-and-answer sessions, some of which were held in front of observers. He didn't seem to know anything about himself that the group hadn't already made up, but he *did* provide some accurate information about real seventeenth-century people and events.

Now, it's worth noting that none of the group really *believed* that Philip was an actual entity—it was assumed that he was a result of their own invention. And, though other groups tried similar experiments with similar results throughout the 1970s, the results can hardly be called conclusive, and it's always possible that there was a hoaxer present. Still, the results do serve to suggest, if not prove, that there's something to the notion that concentrated mental energy can create some sort of physical impact. It also sort of suggests that these impacts can manifest in a way that makes them seem to have a sort of intelligence about them.

So there you have it: ghosts are impressions made on your brain by "living thoughts projected into space." Some of those imprints may be "stronger" and easier to notice than others, and sometimes you simply may not be in the right frame of mind for your brain to pick up on it at all, but the energy is always there, waiting to be reacted to. We can even apply this idea to hauntings that we think we've debunked—the rattling sound may just be the tree brushing against the window, but it was that residual energy that made you *think* that sound was a ghost, rather than just going straight for thinking of the tree. When, in A *Christmas Carol*, Scrooge tells the ghost of Marley that he's not real, just the result of an undigested bit of beef, perhaps Marley could have said, "Well, you're on the right track, there—it was that bit of beef that put you in the right sort of state of mind to see me!"

That's one theory anyway. And while it's pretty sensible compared to some of the stranger theories that go around, it won't explain away every ghost. For instance, if ghosts are all in our heads, why can audio recorders and cameras sometimes seem to pick them up, seeing as how the equipment doesn't have a mind of its own (as much as it sometimes seems to)?

And, anyway, it's sort of a cop-out explanation to say that it really is ghosts making you think the tree brushing against the window is the sound of a gallows being erected. It's like looking at a ghostly figure in a picture, determining that the figure is just an optical illusion created by dust and shadows, but deciding that ghosts use dust and shadows to manifest. Then again, is that so unreasonable? Maybe that *is* how it works.

Once again, no theory can explain *all* ghosts away. And just because mental energy might be able to create a "ghost," it doesn't necessarily mean that some sort of spirit doesn't fly out of a person's nose at the moment of death and embark upon an eternity of rattling chains.

After refreshing myself on the theories that appealed to skeptical minds, I decided it was only fair to find out some of the more paranormal theories.

Luckily, I had a friend who was a psychic detective.

Coffee with a Psychic

In *Sherlock Holmes and the Sign of the Four*, Dr. Watson gives Sherlock Holmes a pocket watch. Holmes looks at it for a second and quickly determines that the watch belonged to Watson's father and then was inherited by his older brother, who was well-to-do, fell in and out of good fortune, and drank himself to death. Watson is furious and assumes that Holmes has been making inquiries into Watson's family history. But Holmes explains that he figured it all out more or less scientifically; the initials engraved on it match it to Watson's family, and he can assume that it would pass to the firstborn son when the owner died. The scratches on the face indicated that Watson's brother was well-to-do enough that he could carelessly carry an expensive watch around in the same pocket as his keys, the dents around the winding-hole indicated that he may have gotten drunk and missed the hole with the key a lot, and the tiny numbers scratched into the inside showed that it was pawned and repurchased repeatedly.

Holmes was right about everything, but he conceded that a lot of it was just instinct on his part that happened to be correct. Holmes never claimed any psychic ability, but he probably could have gotten away with it if he had wanted to. The difference between psychic ability and "instincts" really comes down to little more than good old semantics.

Ken describes himself as clairsentient—he can't see or hear ghosts any more than the rest of us can, but he can sort of sense them. This is distinct from the abilities of clairvoyants, who see things, and clairaudients, who hear things.

But Ken never claims any intimate knowledge of the spirit world or anything (unless he's in the midst of one of his arguments with Hector, during which all bets are off), and, after an initial period of raising my eyebrows at him, I ended up giving him the benefit of the doubt. After all, I saw him in action quite a bit. I saw him talk to people and suddenly know which army unit they'd served in, where they'd served, and where they were injured. If you take him into a haunted graveyard, even one he's never heard of, he can walk around and tell you which graves are said to be haunted with a pretty high rate of accuracy. Even if I chalk it up to Sherlock Holmes–style detective work on his part, it's a pretty remarkable skill. Indeed, he doesn't claim that there is anything "supernatural" about his abilities at all—it's just really good instincts.

After months of working as a guide and not quite feeling that I'd gotten to the bottom of all of the ghost business, but after deciding to give Ken the benefit of the doubt, I sat down with him at his apartment and asked him to explain all of the psychic stuff to me.

When you imagine a psychic's house, you picture crystal balls, soft red and blue lights, or at least some beads hanging down in a doorway. Ken has his fair share of skeleton and monster figurines and books on the occult, but such things are outnumbered in his apartment by the video-game paraphernalia. Dogs and cats run around all over. Rarely are there flashing lights in evidence. He does have some broomsticks, cauldrons, and other stuff that you would expect to find in an apartment rented by pagans, though.

"So, that's all it is?" I asked, as we sat at his kitchen table, watching a black cat (of course) jumping around on the countertops. "Better instincts?"

"Well, I think that 'psychic ability' is a big misnomer, to begin with," he said. "People associate it with the supernatural, which means that it's above and beyond nature. I think it's just the opposite; I think it's within nature. I think that everybody has psychic ability. Women, in particular, seem to be a little bit more adept at it than men. Kids are better than adults. With most people, it's just a fluke—like people who have good artistic ability or good athletic ability. And there are certain professions where you *use* your instincts on a daily basis. Like being in sales. Police detectives use it when they're trying to solve crimes. My ability is just something that is just like that, only a bit more intense. I think that one of the main reasons that people tend not to believe in psychics, though, is that there *are* a lot of fakes out there."

Ken then rattled off a list of well-known TV psychics that he believed had given the real ones a bad name.

"So, how do you tell the difference?" I asked. "Besides just spotting the tricks that fake psychics have been using for hundreds of years?"

"Accuracy." said Ken. "Straight-up accuracy. If what they say comes to fruition." He paused to get one of his black cats off of the counter.

"You witches and your black cats!" I chuckled.

"What it comes down to," he said, sitting back down and pouring some coffee, "is that psychics are just normal people. I can't read your mind any more than your mailman can read your mind. In fact, he's probably *more* likely to know what's going on in your head, because he knows what kind of pornography comes to your house. But the point is, people pooh-pooh this stuff because there are all these phonies with goofy names running around. I mean, I don't show up for a reading saying that my name is Thundering Howling Coyote Six-Finger Monkey Man. I'm just Ken. And it's the same thing in the ghost community—people expect ghost-hunting groups to be a bunch of weirdos with a funny group name. You and I are a big exception, in that we're just Ken, Adam, and sometimes Troy."

"Unless we're calling ourselves Captain Spooky McGuffin and his Paranormal Posse," I said.

"I know, right?" he said with a laugh. "But that's still less corny than most of the group names out there. Same thing happens in the pagan community."

Ken, for the record, is a witch. You meet a lot of witches, Wiccans, and other varieties of pagans when you hang out with geeks (even in Georgia), and find that paganism is just a religion about like any other,[12] and pagan groups are subject to the same drama and infighting as any other religious group. And, just as in the ghost-hunting community, there are a lot of flaky types who give the more levelheaded pagans a bad name. I believe that the "flaky" ones are referred to as "Glindas" in the pagan community.

"So," I asked, "if all of this is just normal, what goes on in your brain that maybe doesn't go on in the other guy's brain?"

"Well, there are a couple of theories about that," he said. "There have been a whole series of studies that were done on what makes psychic people more psychic. One of the things that they found that's quite common is that a lot of people who have high psi ability also happen to have seizure

---

12. Paganism and witchcraft, for the record, really aren't much different from most mainstream religions—the modern forms draw from a variety of ancient, earth-based religions. There's no demon worship or animal sacrifice going on. Some of my best friends are pagans.

disorders. That's one thing. So are people who are color-blind and people who are borderline diabetic."

"Like you," I said. Ken was all three of those.

He nodded. "One of the other things that we've found, and this has nothing to do with me in particular, but people who have extreme diets also tend to have higher psi ability. There are, say, Eskimo shamans that have a diet that consists almost solely of meat, and we find that they have a high psi ability. Same with people who are complete vegans. We don't know why that is. People who play games more have higher psi ability, because they're using and stretching their psychic muscles. One of the things that I do when I teach my class on psychic development is talk to people about playing board games instead of video games, because they're always trying to outguess their opponent in board games."

"So, say, Battleship is essentially a psychic contest?"

"Absolutely," Ken said, getting back up to get the cat off of the counter again. His psychic powers certainly did not give him clairvoyance enough to guess what the cat was going to do next. Hector and I used to pick on him over this sort of thing all the time. If the bus blew a tire or if one of the pubs on the route turned out to be closed on any given night, we'd say, "Boy, Ken, bet you didn't see *that* one coming!" and we'd all have a good laugh—Ken included.

"Now, you come from a long line of psychics, right?" I asked.

"As far back as I can trace," he said. "My grandfather, Don Melvoin, was a TV personality in Traverse City, Michigan. He played both Count Zapula, the local horror show host, and Deputy Dan, the kids' show host. He was also a psychic. His speciality was psychometry, which means he got information from objects. He'd hold an item in his hand and pick up things like emotional content. I also had a great-grandmother who never claimed to be a psychic, but she did teach me how to read a crystal ball. And I think that one of the ways this helped me develop as a psychic was that my parents treated it as perfectly normal. Kids tend to be more psychic than adults, like I said, and a lot of parents really praise kids when they predict things, or when weird things happen. And the kids want praise, so they will just start to get creative. On the other side, really religious parents might see it as satanic and try to suppress it. But in my family, it was just normal."

Ken went on to tell me that some of his earliest psychic experiences were predicting the deaths of family members, which made him pretty popular at family gatherings. Later, he continued to develop his ability while studying under Irene Hughes, the famous psychic who predicted the assassinations of both John and Robert Kennedy, the death of Howard Hughes (who was not a relative of hers, but was a client), and the Chicago Blizzard of 1967. She was apparently very famous in psychic circles, but I didn't recall ever having heard of her personally. I asked Ken what he learned from her.

"Oh, Irene is wonderful," he said. "She contacted me to come to work at her psychic fairs right at a time when I was looking to move out of Detroit to Chicago. Which was awesome, because Detroit is a shithole, except for the fact that it has great radio stations. She's one of the only people I've ever seen who can walk into a casino, pick a slot machine, and come out with five thousand bucks."

I raised my eyebrows. One thing that we skeptics say all the time is that no one's ever found a psychic who could break the bank at Vegas. Ken himself opened most tours by assuring people that he didn't know what the lottery numbers were.

"So, she'd use her psychic instinct to figure out which slot machine to use?"

"She used numerology more than instincts. A lot of number crunching with a little bit of intuition thrown in. I mean, when I teach astrology or numerology, I sort of describe it as the algebra of life. We can say that the moon has some sort of gravitational effect on people's moods and the weather, but we can't say what that effect is. So, the effect is sort of x. It's all algebra."

I've never been a big believer in astrology—or even a little one. Ken worked it all out for me as a form of number crunching. It wasn't enough to make me start reading horoscopes or asking people what their sign was, but it was at least a fairly coherent explanation.

"So, now you've been doing readings for twenty years, including a lot of rock stars and celebrities," I said, before Ken could say another word about algebra. "Any juicy gossip?"

He shook his head. "Really, celebrities want to know the same stuff as everyone else. Love, health … all of the usual crap."

"Come on," I pressed. "Hasn't there been any crazy celebrity that has really freaked you out?"

He paused, smiled, and brought up the name of a certain rock star.

"She freaked me out so much that I wouldn't do a reading for her," he said. "I flat out refused the second she walked into the room. Her aura was just … the only way I can describe it is that she had this aura of being as slimy as two eels having sex in a bucket of snot."

He asked me not to name any names, but this is also just about the way most non-psychics describe this particular rock star.

"Now," I said, "you've also worked with police forces on murder investigations and things like that, right?"

He nodded.

"What leads them to seek out a psychic rather than doing normal detective work?

"Usually frustration," Ken said. "They run out of regular clues or leads, so they'll call me and ask for help pointing them in a way that'll lead them to another clue or a piece of evidence that they need in order to go for the conviction. I'll get as little information as possible and go into a sort of a delta-theta state, a meditative state, and see what

I come up with. Like, I might say, 'There are two Native American men and one woman, and a gray pickup truck with rust spots. You'll find something under the lumber in the truck.' And it'll turn out that that matches the suspects they have in custody, and one of their friends will have a truck like that with bloodstains in the back."

Ken has done this many times. For a time he was part of a group of psychics that would get blind e-mails about missing persons. These psychics would send back whatever information came to them, and cases would be built based on any consensus that was reached. The success rate was very high, but egos and politics got involved, as they usually do in things like that, and the group fell apart. He's been trying to restart it ever since. At the time of the interview, he'd helped on about twenty different cases with law enforcement agencies all over the country and even internationally. All of this work was done off the record and was entirely pro bono.

"Now, what's all this about a delta-theta state?" I asked. That's what I wanted to get into—the science, or at least the pseudoscience, behind psychic ability. If, as Ken insisted, all of this ghost and psychic stuff was totally natural, not supernatural, it stood to reason that there should at least be some scientific theories to attempt to explain how it worked.

"Well," he said, "hang on. Let me get my cheat sheet." He disappeared into his office and came back with a printout with various numbers on it.

"You see," he said, "there are electrochemical signals that travel through the brain, with a rate of speed measured in cycles per second. Fourteen to twenty-eight cycles per second are called beta waves, which is the speed of the brain at normal consciousness. Eight to thirteen cycles per second are beta waves, which is the subconscious. Four to seven are theta waves, and below that are the waves generated during a really deep sleep."

This made sense to me. After all, I'd just found out the rate at which eyeballs vibrate. I didn't have any data of my own to tell about electromechanical signals in the brain, but this all seemed reasonable enough.

"The delta-theta state is sort of a state between asleep and awake. It's like ... have you ever had a dream where you were trying to scream, and woke up almost screaming? Or woke up feeling like there was a fat guy on your chest?"

"Yes!" I said. "Just the other night!"

Recently, I had had a dream about trying to look up a story I'd heard years ago about a headless ghost who wandered around singing, "Tiptoe Through the Tulips." In the dream, I was trying to find the story online, and I kept coming across images of ghostly old women that were so frightening I could hardly look at them. No ghosts are quite so scary as old lady ghosts, if you ask me.

I woke up feeling as though I were pinned to the bed by an unseen force; in particular, there was a distinct pressure on my chest. Even in my half-awake state, I remembered that this was a fairly common form of ghost sighting—

waking up with the feeling of pressure on the chest. Often, these reports seem to be connected to ghostly old ladies. Like the scary ones in my dream.

But I remember thinking, as I lay there feeling the pressure, *This isn't really so bad. It just feels like someone's set up a laptop computer on my chest. As long as I don't open my eyes and see the scary old lady, I'm gonna be all right!*

When the feeling went away and I became more alert and awake, I thought of a few more rational explanations. The most obvious solution was that I'd been awakened by the cat walking onto my chest and sitting down. The next-most obvious is that I was still half asleep and still dreaming the whole thing.

It may well be that neither of these is actually correct. But, from a strictly rational point of view, there are an awful lot of explanations that make more sense than blaming it on a ghostly old lady. It's even more rational to suppose that my roommate had, in a moment of severe drunkenness, decided to set up a laptop on my chest and get some typing done. He *did* do some strange things when he drank.

In fact, on further research, there turned out to be a lot I didn't know about the "old hag" experience—suffering from it is common enough to have given rise to the term "hagridden" for those who have suffered from it. Traditionally, it was attributed to having an old hag sitting on your chest, sending bad dreams into your head. Today, it's known as sleep paralysis—no one knows exactly what causes it, but it does seem to be a form of hallucination, triggered by any number of reactions of various brain tissues and synapses to the REM sleep state. Most commonly, it's suspected to be due to a lack of melatonin. A lack of melatonin can lead to a lack of depolarization, the process that keeps you from moving your body as you move around in dreams (i.e., if you're running a race in your dreams but not flailing your legs around and kicking the crap out of your sleeping spouse, you have depolarization to thank). No one knows for sure, but, as I expected, there were plenty more rational explanations going around that I should consider before blaming the whole thing on a ghostly old hag sitting on me (and thank goodness for that).

I described this whole chain of events to Ken.

"Well," he said, "what you were in when you woke up, not quite awake but not quite asleep, was a delta-theta state. And that's the state that we induce to sort of tune into psychic stuff."

This was also, I noted, the kind of state in which Dr. Bernard Hollander had said people were more likely to pick up on those "living thoughts projected into space by the personality."

"All right," I said. "Now here's the real issue. How does all of this relate to ghosts? Are there brain waves that sort of create ghosts or allow you to be in tune with them?"

Ken took a deep breath, then went to get the cat off the counter again. This, I knew, was a loaded question, as almost all questions about ghosts and the theories behind them are.

"Well," he said, "There's a current metaphysical theory that the thing that ties the body and the soul together—the soul, for lack of a better term—is our consciousness, our intellect, and our emotional content. That's what our soul is. How that ties into the body is the spirit. The spirit, we think, lives in the blood, so when it's spilled, it leaves an energy residue behind that could either be picked up by certain sensitive instruments, or it can be picked up by certain types of sensitive people."

He paused and poured some coffee. "Have you worked with any other psychics before?"

I shook my head. "Not really," I said, "unless you count the ones that we get on the tour."

We got a lot of self-proclaimed psychics on the tour, many of whom were pretty clearly just senile or who wanted to be psychics so badly that they had convinced themselves that they were. Under Ken's theory that everyone is psychic, I suppose we could say that they were, but they pretty clearly didn't know what they were doing. Hector and I had a whole system—when someone claimed to be psychic, we'd make up a ghost and see if they could "really feel" that one. Most of them failed miserably, but at least none of them ever pulled a piece of cheesecloth out of their butt and told me it was ectoplasm, which I suppose is progress.

Troy did say, though, that he'd once worked with a psychic on an investigation who said that the only way to get the fairies out of a haunted barn was to roll around in horse dung, so we can't have progressed *that* far from the ectoplasm days.

"You see," said Ken, "this is where I differ from most of them on investigations. They'll sense an energy or something, but since they're not that well trained, they won't really know how to analyze it, and they'll just start making stuff up. Remember that guy at Odin Tatu?"

Recently, a TV crew had brought a supposed psychic through Odin Tatu, which remained open—and haunted—after Tapeworm's death under the name of Old Town Tatu. The people there had set the psychic up by asking him trick questions, and he'd failed. He *had* said that he was hearing the f-word an awful lot—which sure sounded like the ghost of Tapeworm—but, for the most part, according to Ken, he was probably just reacting to the energy in the room and making up stories to go with it.

"So, if these people are picking up on energy, what kind of energy is this, and how does it get there?"

"There are different theories, of course," he said. "But what happens is that emotional energy is like any other energy; it can't be destroyed.[13] And strong emotions can sometimes leave an emotional residue—that psychic imprint

13. This is basic science—the three rules of thermodynamics are: 1. Energy can never be created, only spent or transformed. 2. All actions use some energy. 3. Energy can never be completely depleted. This is often summarized as "You can't win, you can't break even, and you can't get out of the game."

stuff that we talk about. And untrained psychics will mistake this for a ghost. A good example of this is the Anne Frank house in the Netherlands, which I investigated. If you know the story of Anne Frank, you'll know that nobody died in that house, but a lot of people think it's haunted. What happens is that people go through there and feel bad about the Holocaust, about the Nazis, and about what happened in the Netherlands. And that leaves behind this emotional residue, and people pick up on it and *think* it's a ghost."

"So, sometimes what we call a haunting might have been *caused* by a dead guy, but it isn't actually a dead guy in the room?"

"Absolutely," he said. "The Eastland is a good example of this."

There did seem to be emotional residue, or whatever you call it, at that site. Lots of people had reported walking over the bridges near the site and being overcome by a profound sense of sadness and sorrow—oddly, high school groups always wanted to try walking across the bridge to see if they could feel it. I was always amused by how eager they were to feel profound sadness. Kids nowadays!

"See," said Ken, "at the Eastland site, it's sort of six of one, half a dozen of the other. There are ghosts there *and* that emotional residue. The first time I was there, to be honest, it was awful. It was one of the worst-feeling places that I had ever been to in my life, outside of Dachau concentration camp. And to go there on a regular basis, like I do, I have to sort of shut it down. That's part of why I never do readings on the tour. If you're at a place where 844 people died in a terrible tragedy, you don't want to open yourself up to that emotionally. I don't know if that makes sense to anybody, but people who are a little bit sensitive can understand it."

"So," I said, "are some of the ghosts that are actually seen or photographed possibly ghosts caused by this emotional residue from people who are still alive?"

"Sure," he said. "That happens a lot. You've heard stories of that—people waking up seeing an image of their brother and finding out their brother had just been in a terrible car accident on the other side of the world. That's emotional energy, not a ghost, in and of itself."

What we had reached was the ultimate question: what counts as a ghost and what doesn't? To me, this emotional residue stuff was fine to count as a ghost, especially when it manifested as a vision of a dead person. To Ken, it was only actual, intelligent, independent spirits that really, truly counted.

"Now, one last tough one," I said. "Let's talk about when psychics are wrong."

No psychic is always right—even Irene Hughes only claimed about 80 percent accuracy.

"Well," said Ken, "it can be really hard to tell the difference sometimes between actual psychic intuition and just second-guessing myself based on regular instinct. And, naturally, sometimes I'm going to be wrong. Like, a few years ago, I actually made some phone calls to the FBI saying I thought that there was about to be a terrorist bombing in Atlanta. And there wasn't. And some people suggested that maybe my calls led them to stop it from happening, but I'm totally sure that I was just wrong. But you know, I love this country. I think our diversity makes us the greatest country in the world. And there are all these self-proclaimed psychics who are saying that they predicted 9/11, but didn't say anything because they were afraid they'd look foolish. And I think they should be considered traitors. I'm willing to make a fool of myself. Heck, I'm *great* at making a fool of myself!"

"You got that right," I said. And we had a good laugh. When Ken and I ran podcasts or investigations or tours together, we had a really nifty dynamic in which Ken would be the "believer" and I would try to reel him in with logical explanations for things. I was, if you will, Scully to his Mulder. Sometimes I'd score a point on him, and sometimes he'd score one on me. Ken and I are living proof that skeptics and psychics don't have to try to shout each other down. We can, in fact, learn from one another and live and work together in peace.

Abandoned by All but the Ghosts (and Ghost Hunters)

Our investigative team was a good one, even when it was just the two of us, Ken and me, on an investigation. We didn't have ranks, demerits, and uniforms like some ghost-hunting groups; some say that that sort of thing helps them appear to be more professional, but it seems to me more like an excuse to get egos involved.

Sometimes we used a lot of gear, sometimes we didn't. Exactly what kind of gear you should use on a ghost hunt is the subject of a whole *lot* of debate, but the bottom line is that we don't really know. Logically, which equipment will work best ought to vary on a ghost-by-ghost basis. Really, you can use *anything*. On a ghost hunt, any sort of equipment that gets a weird reading tends to be held up as evidence of a ghost being nearby, whether it's a radio station losing its signal or an EMF reader showing a jump.

My specialty became EVP—"electronic voice phenomena"—the practice of wandering around with a microphone to see if any ghostly voices or sounds could be recorded. It wasn't because of any great belief in the technique; I just became the EVP guy because in my years of playing in bands (and occasionally bootlegging rock concerts), I had accumulated a bunch of good portable recording gear. It was sort of like getting a job as a drummer because you happen to have a drum. But I got to be pretty good at it, if I do say so myself, and we got some cool recordings now and then.

But the most important part of our job, the part that paid the bills, wasn't the investigations (only quacks really make money on those); it was the tour business. It wasn't a huge moneymaker either—it didn't pay enough for anyone to live on, but it helped me survive without having to get another retail job.

I even worked to promote business. I had never, ever had a job that I would have promoted before—usually, I would recommend people *not* shop at whatever store I worked at. But I worked hard to promote Chicago Spooks—for once in my life, it was in my best interest for a company to stay in business. Whereas I knew that Starbucks would be just fine no matter how bad a job I did, Chicago Spooks' fortune actually depended, somewhat, on me.

So I promoted them. I had a "Ghostbuster" jacket made, and whenever someone complimented me on it, I'd say, "It's actually my night job!" and hand them a flier. In the summer, around the time that we first investigated Odin Tatu, I even started a sort of a carnival barker routine to drum up business. Troy designed a flier, Olga had several hundred printed up, and on evenings when Ken was running the tour, I'd go to the Oriental Theatre, the site of the old Iroquois Theater, when crowds were arriving to see *Wicked*, which was playing an open-ended run there.

"Consider the ghost tour, ladies and gentlemen!" I would shout in my best vaudeville voice. "See what happened right here in 1903 only on the ghost tour! If you like witches, you'll love ghosts! Step right up, ladies and gentlemen, it's fun for the whole family on the ghost tour! Most educational tour in the city, guaranteed! Don't let the tourists know more about your neighborhood than you do! Take the ghost tour!"

I'd keep this up for about twenty minutes until the bus rolled by, then for another several minutes I'd yammer on outside of the bus itself. The bus would arrive right around the time the show started, so the crowds would be thinning out. When Ken led the people off the bus and into Death Alley, I'd stick around and chat with Hector or Willie for a minute.

Hector and I would goof around a lot. One day, after I showed him my "barker" voice and listened to him give me a lecture on carnival history to show me that "barker" was a derogatory term, we both started talking like guys in a movie about 1900-era newsies as the people filed back to the bus. I don't remember why, but I suppose it seemed like a good idea at the time.

"You know, Silas," said Hector to me, "I hear that Troy Taylor's going to be running a supernatural tour!"

"Is that right, Amos?" I replied. "Speaking of the supernatural, do you know Ken the Medium? He says that this new theater is going to burn down on December thirtieth!"

"Never!" Hector scoffed. "Medium schmedium! Hasn't he seen the ads? This theater is absolutely fireproof!"

I'm not sure whether anyone else found this funny, but the fact that we were having a good time showed—and when we had a good time, the people on the tours had a good time.

I'd worked enough jobs over the years that I knew just how valuable it was to have a good crew that got along well and had complementary skills. Ken, Troy, Hector, Willie, and I were the best team I'd ever been on. Ken and Hector argued like crazy, but there wasn't any drama behind it—they just tended to bicker like brothers. We were giving fantastic tours, finding information and stories that had never been featured on ghost tours in the city before, and building a truly solid reputation.

Of course, such good things can't last.

One day I was walking up to Milwaukee Avenue to take the bus downtown to pass fliers around and came across Ken, who was driving the ghost bus up to the pickup spot on Clark Street. I waved, and he slowed down and picked me up.

"I'm afraid I have some bad news," he said, as we drove down Chicago Avenue. "Ray's getting out of jail."

"Who's Ray?" I asked.

I hadn't heard the story of Ray yet.

Ray, Olga's husband, had been one of the main tour guides for the company in 2004. He had served about six months of a three-year sentence in prison for arson and was being paroled.

"So, what's going to happen?" I asked Ken.

"I don't know," said Ken. "But Olga's probably going to be getting back together with him, and I think they might just start doing all of the tours themselves and restart the company from scratch."

"What should we do?" I asked. "Do you think we ought to buy them out or something?"

"I don't know," said Ken. "We'll wait and see, I guess."

"Come on, Ken!" I said. "You're the psychic here! Why wait and see?"

We both had a good chuckle, but we couldn't cover the fact that we were nervous. This was the best job I'd ever had, the only job—other than writing smart-ass children's books—that I'd ever been good at, and now I was not only in danger of losing it, I was going to have to start dealing with the kind of guy who set fires at churches.

Ray got out right around the day we first investigated Odin Tatu. That day, he shouted out various unprintable names at Olga while she spoke to the press about supposed hauntings at Wrigley Field.[14]

Hector and I were making plans for how to deal with Ray if he ever showed up and tried to commandeer the bus, most of which involved crafty ninja moves that were just crazy enough to work. I spoke to Troy about what we should do, but Troy was at a loss, as well.

"I've been warning Olga that I'd quit if he came back, and she keeps telling me he's found Jesus," said Troy. "I'm Catholic, too, and I didn't know Jesus was missing to start with! After that whole thing at Wrigley, Olga called and said, 'I guess you want to say you told me so,' but even I didn't think it would be this fast! I thought it would take a few weeks!"

But, lo and behold, a few weeks later, Ray was in charge of the company and Troy was gone. Troy claimed that he resigned, and Olga claimed to have fired him. I'm still not sure exactly which of those is correct; I suspect it was a little bit of both. Troy had certainly said that he would quit if Ray was back in the picture, and Olga probably said something like, "You can't quit, you're fired!"

---

14. For the record, there aren't any ghosts at Wrigley Field that we know of. The few stories going around about it are nonsense.

Having Ray back changed the dynamics of the company quite a bit. I had only rarely spoken to Olga—we'd chatted on the phone a few times, she and Troy had both come on the St. Patrick's Day Haunted Pub Crawl, and Olga had come on the investigation into the Congress Hotel a couple of months before, but most of my contact over the months that I'd been with the company had been with Troy. He was the one who sent me the passenger lists on the day of the tours, handled the reservations, spoke to me on the phone, and sent me my paychecks.

Ken and I encouraged Troy to start up another tour business of his own in Chicago. Our main worry was simply staying at work—the thought of not being able to keep doing tours was keeping me up at night, and working for Ray didn't seem like it would have a lot of job security. Or any kind of security, for that matter. I knew the guy had paid his debt and all, but there are certain things a guy can threaten to do with a screwdriver that you just can't take too lightly, whether you were the one he threatened or not. I understood that Ray and Troy had even gotten into fisticuffs one night at Hull House.

Eventually, Troy, Ken, and I decided to go into business together. After all, we were putting a lot of effort into research and promotions. Ken and I even planned to start up a podcast as a promotional vehicle. Using this energy to promote a company that we were in control of simply made sense. And, anyway, while Olga paid me reasonably well, the pay was less than 10 percent of what the company

Weird Chicago Bus

grossed on a sold-out tour. This way, we not only made a higher percentage of the funds, we would have more creative control. So we bought ourselves a used school bus, had it fixed up and painted, and founded the Weird Chicago Tour Company.

I thought that calling it "Weird Chicago," rather than having the word "ghost," "spook," or "haunted" right in the name, was an especially good idea, as it was a lot less limiting. When you have a company with the word "ghost" in it, you sort of have to run ghost tours and nothing else. Doing anything else would be like being in The Beach Boys and trying to play music other than surf music (which they had a lot of trouble trying to do). Weird Chicago, we decided, would specialize in ghost tours, but also offer any number of specialty historical tours that would take advantage of all of the research we were doing.

There was another issue, too—being in charge would allow us to become the "good" ghost people. Ken and I still felt as though we should repeat stories in Olga's books and stories we'd gotten from Ray, including those that we were pretty sure weren't true when we ran Chicago Spooks tours. We were also telling a lot of stories that were popular legends in Chicago but which, we had found, didn't have even the slightest basis in fact.

I didn't mind telling ghost stories that may not have been true (there's no way to tell most of the time, after all), and all tour guides distort the facts a bit when convenient. As the saying goes, "When the legend is better than the fact, print the legend," though I tried to at least *know* the facts in case anyone really wanted to know. But I felt like we could at least try our best to get the historical parts of the stories right. Very few tour companies of any sort put a lot of effort into that sort of thing, honestly, but sketchy historical research is especially rampant in the ghost business. I don't want to name names, but I can name quite a few well-known writers of "true ghost stories" who made up at least a few of their best stories, and Troy can name quite a few more.

Starting our own company allowed us to go back to square one, even on the stories that we had memorized, and get all of the facts straight (or closer to it, anyway). We ended up finding out a lot of stuff that was actually quite a bit more interesting—and spookier—than the stuff that had been made up over the years.

But Ken and I still intended to keep running tours for Chicago Spooks at the time—after all, the route was solid, the team was great, and the tours we were giving were the best in town. And I had no official contract with Chicago Spooks—there was never a bit of paperwork, in fact. I was, as far as I was concerned, a "freelance historically based supernatural education consultant."

That October, I worked double duty, doing Weird Chicago tours on weekends and Chicago Spooks during the week. I think I was doing an average of about ten tours per week that October, often on large charter buses where the microphone didn't work.

Soon, my throat was absolutely ravaged. I tried just about every cure for sore vocal cords known to science— slippery elm tea, tequila (which made for some very interesting tours), straight lemon juice, even a warm mixture of brandy and water. (I noticed that people in books by Charles Dickens drank brandy and water a lot, and *they* sure seemed to be able to talk at great length without their voices wearing out.) Nothing really worked that well. I usually sounded like I'd been gargling shrapnel by the end of the tour.

Since my voice was so wrecked, I experimented, very briefly, with doing tours "theatrically" or "in character." A lot of ghost tours are run by guys dressed like they're working at the Haunted Mansion at Disney World. They often swing lanterns around and, on occasion, talk in fake accents. Quite a few customers expect me to show up dressed as a Victorian undertaker. But keeping this act up in a small group for three hours didn't work; it got silly after about five minutes, especially on daytime tours. It might work better on nighttime walking tours, I suppose—some of the tours around the country that do things theatrically put on a very good show.

But I wasn't trying to "put on a show" on either Weird Chicago or Chicago Spooks—we wanted to be entertaining, but we weren't a theatrical tour. There were no special effects or guys in costumes lying in wait to jump out at people in Death Alley. Also, my credibility as a researcher and investigator was important; it's hard for anyone to take you all that seriously when you're speaking in a fake British accent.

During this period, my dealings with Ray were all more or less fine; he went out of his way to be about as professional as possible, at least in my experience. But when Olga found out that Ken and I were still going to work with Troy, she flipped and started to call Ken and I, demanding that we pick one side or the other. Ray was even quoting the Bible at Ken, which is a sort of unusual way to persuade a pagan to do something.

As much as I hated being in the middle of a tug-of-war between the two companies, it was also rather flattering. In the twelve years since I'd joined the workforce as a fourteen-year-old grocery bagger, I'd certainly never been in a situation in which employers would argue over me. I wasn't a very good bagger, my services as a busboy and waiter were easily replaceable, and, though I was a pretty good Starbucks barista, if I do say so myself, my distinct lack of company loyalty made me a poor candidate for management. Being fought over felt awfully nice.

Olga told us flat out that we had to pick one company or the other—we could either work for her and Ray or for Troy, but not both of them. We both kept working for Chicago Spooks through October, so as not to leave them high and dry during the busy season, then switched over to devote all of our energy to Weird Chicago.

We hired Willie as a driver, but Hector stayed with Chicago Spooks and became one of their regular guides. As we were afraid would happen, though, they fired him after about a year. Hector ended up drifting out of the ghost business altogether.

Owning a third of our new bus made me a vehicle owner for the first time in years—I'd sold my car when I moved to Chicago, where cars aren't really necessary, since most things are accessible either by walking or via public transit. Ken hadn't owned a car in even longer. But having a bus certainly had its advantages—not only did it make it a whole lot easier for me to buy large quantities of groceries now and then, Ken and I realized right away that we could use it to investigate places outside of the city limits that were hard to access on the train. Neither of us owned a car—most of our investigations were carried out within the Chicago city limits (which, of course, kept us busy enough). We celebrated our newfound freedom by taking a trip to Bachelor's Grove cemetery.

Bachelor's Grove, a small cemetery in the middle of the Rubio Woods Forest Preserve in the suburb of Midlothian, is sometimes called the most haunted cemetery in the world. If it's not the most haunted, it's certainly among the most vandalized. Most of the gravestones have vanished over the years. Those that remain are often broken, illegible, or spray-painted over. In the 1970s, when police apparently didn't even know it existed, it was an ideal place for teenagers to hold clandestine keggers, being small, out-of-the-way, and the subject of any number of local legends. I'm always a bit wary of haunted places that were once kegger sites (drunks tend to see *lots* of ghosts, per Selzer's First Theorem), but the stories about Bachelor's Grove were widespread enough, and cool enough, to attract my interest.

In fact, the stories about it were scary enough that, for a while, on my tours with Hector, they were the "closer," the last thing I'd talk about on the tour, guaranteed to leave the people freaked out. When asked why we weren't going there, I had a standard response:

"There are three reasons. Number one," I'd say, as Hector held up one finger, "it's about an hour and a half away with the traffic. Number two," Hector's second finger would go up, "it's illegal to be there after dark, and cops tend to crack down on people who sneak in there at night these days. And number three," Hector raised a third finger, "neither Hector nor I would be caught *dead* in that place after dark!"

"No way!" Hector would say, emphatically. "When you walk up to that place, you just hear this voice in your head that says 'Leave!' over and over again!"

People on the bus who had been there—and quite a few had—would nod their heads in agreement. At this point, I had never actually been there myself—as far away as it was, getting there by public transportation was more trouble than it was worth, and, on another level, though I was pretty much over my old fear of cemeteries, the idea of going into one myself still felt like a bad idea.

Now, normally, Ken and I would explain to people that we knew of no good reason that cemeteries ought to be haunted, since ghosts normally haunt the places where they died, and very few people die in cemeteries. But we do hear about a lot of haunted graveyards, and it follows that the kind of ghosts who *do* get reported in cemeteries tend to be very unusual ghosts. While Bachelor's Grove has its own requisite woman in white who wanders among the graves and the usual ghost lights that are seen floating around (with the peculiar variation that one particular blue orb that is seen around the cemetery seems to have some form of intelligence about it that enables it to follow people around), there are lots of really bizarre ghosts that are seen around the cemetery and the adjacent pond, such as the ghost of a two-headed man that is seen walking around. And, of course, there's my personal favorite—the ghost of a house.

Some people will swear that there used to be a house nearby the cemetery—a white Victorian farmhouse with a porch and a porch swing that could be heard to creak. Plenty of people claim to have seen it. I've even had people on the tours who claim to have had picnics outside of it when they were children.

There are two strange things about these stories: for one thing, no two witnesses seem to agree on *where* the house was in relation to the cemetery. It's been reported all over the surrounding woods. For another, according to any property records, no such house ever existed. There are foundations of a few houses in the woods, but they all appear to have been far smaller than the house people describe.

One story that goes around is that the house once belonged to a caretaker who began to hear voices in the graveyard telling him to kill his family. People who hear voices like that tend to be a bit unbalanced to start with, and this guy, according to the stories, was unbalanced enough to do what they told him. He killed his family with a pitchfork, then hanged himself from a nearby tree. When the deed was discovered, the townspeople tore down the house and erased all traces that it had ever existed from the record. It's a pretty unlikely story, but in the 1800s it was probably still possible for a town to pull off a stunt like that.

There are plenty more modern legends about the cemetery, like stories of bodies being dug up by vandals and dumped, along with the tombstones, into the adjacent pond.

Inevitably, there are stories that Al Capone used the pond as a dumping ground for people he had murdered. It wouldn't be a Chicago story if we couldn't work Uncle Al into it.

Stories even abound as to how it came to be known as Bachelor's Grove. There are three prevailing theories: One is that it was initially a burial ground for bachelors. Another is that it was once a plot of land where some psychotic woman used to murder bachelors (this, in particular, is believed by practically no one). The other is that the plot of land was initially owned by the Batchelder family, and the name simply changed to "bachelor" over the years.[15]

Ken needed to take a trip out there to refamiliarize himself with it—he was scheduled to do a nighttime investigation there with a newspaper reporter (and, for the sake of legality, the Midlothian sheriff) for a Halloween issue, so we decided to test out the bus and take a trip down there on an early October morning.

Even our drive to get there was rather eventful—the directions I had were pretty bad (apparently, they were directions to get there from Gary, Indiana, not from Chi-

---

15. There doesn't seem to be any documentary evidence or records to back this up, but, interestingly, while doing genealogical research, I ran across an ancestor of mine named Abigail Batchelder who lived in Salem, Massachusetts, in the late 1600s. Some of the other Batchelders in the area, as it turns out, served as jurors and witnesses in the famous witch trials. If we could connect these guys, or their descendants, to the area, we'd have a fantastic built-in explanation for why the place is so haunted. Salem is a great town for ghost tours and stories, despite the fact that no one executed there was *actually* a witch, or even a pagan. They were just unpopular people who didn't fit in.

cago, which led us to come pretty close to Wisconsin before realizing we were going the wrong way). Then, as we
drove down Cicero Avenue (which goes through some awfully bad neighborhoods), the muffler fell off of the bottom of the bus. It was as though some unseen force—perhaps the one that told people to "Leave"—didn't want us to
go to that cemetery!

Still, after a long, long trip, we parked the bus in the
Rubio Woods Forest Preserve parking lot, crossed over the
Midlothian Turnpike, and jumped over a chain that was
doing a lousy job of blocking a trail that led into the
woods.

It was a gorgeous day for a hike; the leaves were just
starting to change colors. The cemetery was roughly half a
mile down the leafy trail.

The first thing I noticed as we approached the graveyard was the distinct lack of any voice in my head telling
me to leave. In fact, despite my own lingering reluctance
to get within three city blocks of a cemetery, the place
seemed remarkably pleasant to me. The atmosphere of the
place was calm and peaceful—more so, even, than the
woods themselves nearby. It seemed like a lovely place to
have a picnic.

Recently, there had been a lot of efforts to clean up the
cemetery. Weeds had been pulled up, graffiti had been
washed off. Some of the broken tombstones had been set
back up and cleaned. There weren't very many gravestones

Grave at Bachelor's Grove

left in the place—probably not much more than a dozen or so remained. But they didn't look that spooky at all.

Of course, that "haunted vibe" comes and goes. When it's strong at a place, I barely even need to tell a story to freak people out. When it's absolutely not there, the same place won't scare anyone that much, no matter what stories I tell them. On another day, the "vibe" at the cemetery might have been so strong that no one would even go through the gate. On the day we visited, though, it was just plain pleasant in there.

Not quite so pleasant, however, was the famous pond. The pond was covered in scum, algae, and other gunk. It looked as though there were about fifty different diseases floating around in it.

Bachelor's Grove Pond

After wandering around the graveyard for a while, chatting with other people who had come to look for ghosts before the Halloween crowds showed up, we stepped over the fence—a part of which had been destroyed by a falling tree—and wandered through the woods around the cemetery.

The woods—as some people had reported to me—were actually a lot spookier than the cemetery itself. It was there that I felt as though I were being watched, as though someone other than Ken was walking behind me. In one of the little streams that cuts through the woods, Ken found a bole stone—a stone with a hole in it that is sacred to certain pagan religions.[16]

---

16. Elsewhere in the creek, we found an empty film canister full of pot residue, testifying to the fact the graveyard's days as a place to get wasted are far from over.

Finally, after walking across a couple of streams not too far from the graveyard, we came upon the foundation of an old house.

We'd heard about this foundation being in there—a tiny, square-shaped sinkhole, about two feet deep, one side of which is lined with an old stone wall. Near it on one side was an old pipe disappearing into the ground. On the other side were the stone remains of a long-since-filled-in well.

This was only one of a couple of old foundations that exist in the woods, though none of them appear to have been foundations of houses nearly large enough to match the descriptions of the mysterious Victorian farmhouse. What's most odd about them is that bits of evidence of the old structures keep on popping up—though ghost hunters tend to pick up the bits of pipe, stonework, and rubble that were clearly a part of the houses and take them home with them, more and more pieces keep turning up. Indeed, we found a small piece of green, vaguely ornamental piping. Given the number of thrill seekers who tromp around the woods, it seemed impossible that it could have been there for years without anyone picking it up.

Here, I finally felt as spooked as I had expected to feel in the cemetery. My EVP gear, at that moment, picked up the sound of a dog barking—there were certainly no dogs nearby—and a creaking sound, like the creak of an old door. Or a porch swing. Like the one at the mysterious disappearing house. You could hear it pretty clearly on the podcast we recorded.

Other than that, nothing particularly odd happened during that trip to Bachelor's Grove. But two nights later I was at Hull House, running a Chicago Spooks tour with Hector, when the phone rang. It was Ken.

Knowing that Ken wouldn't call me in the middle of a tour unless it was an emergency, I answered. He sounded somewhat freaked out—which, for Ken, is really saying something.

"I'm on that investigation at Bachelor's Grove with the sheriff and the newspaper guy," he said. "And something really weird happened."

I stepped over to the edge of the Garden of Evil and saw that the customers were busily taking pictures and exploring, under Hector's direction, giving me a few minutes to chat.

"What happened?" I asked.

"Well, I was standing over this one grave on the west end of the cemetery, by that tree that fell over onto the fence," he said. "And I felt like my psychic ability just came on like a switch had been turned on. And I started feeling, like, 'There was a kid here. He lost something. He lost some money.' And I started going into a sort of a haze."

The newspaper would later describe that when Ken felt as though a boy had lost something there, he looked as though he had "lost it" himself.

"So, what happened?" I asked.

"Well, I went into that haze, and I just kind of wandered over to the pond and started walking into it," he said.

"Are you crazy?" I asked. "You're gonna need a tetanus shot. And maybe whatever they give people for dysentery!"

"I know," he said. "Actually, I was mostly worried about snapping turtles biting my dick off. But I waded out 'til I was about knee deep, stuck my hand down into the muck at the bottom, and pulled out a Liberty half dollar coin from the forties."

He sounded awfully spooked. My first thought, as a skeptic, was that he must have tossed it in there surreptitiously while we were there together. This was Troy's first reaction, too. However, had he done such a thing, there's no way in hell he would have been able to find it again a minute later, let alone two days later.

I then hit on the notion that it must have been up his sleeve or something—but even then, he could have gotten just as dramatic an effect by burying the thing in the dirt and digging it back up. That would have been just as good a story for the papers, and it would have spared him having to wade into the water—which, even disregarding the stories about bodies being dumped there, can't possibly have been a wise idea. Not only did he risk encountering a snapping turtle with a taste for wieners, he risked contracting any number of the diseases that could practically be seen floating around in the place.

He was especially worried that the newspapers would claim that he had faked it. "I have no way to prove I didn't," he said. "Psychic-bashing is as easy as punching a baby. I almost wish it had never even happened." The newspaper story was to be the first mention of Weird Chicago Tours in the press—neither of us wanted to start out with a reputation as a couple of major bullshitters. We were trying to be the *good* ghost people. The ones that you could trust.

Thankfully, when the story hit the papers, though, the reporter sounded reasonably convinced. Like me, perhaps, he was willing to give Ken the benefit of the doubt.

Meet the Weirdos

I think that after *Meet the Press*, they should have a show called *Meet the Weirdos*. It would feature whatever political yahoo had just been on *Meet the Press* sitting down to chat with a UFO buff, a guy who claims to be a time traveler, and someone who thinks the greatest challenge our nation faces is spandex-clad devil worshippers who wear a lot of eye makeup and embed backward messages into rock songs. That political yahoo would be seeing what it's like to be a figurehead in the ghost industry for a day.

Any skeptic knows that the ghost business is full of real weirdos—the type of people who swear that orb photos are "proof" of the afterlife, or "proof" that everything the Catholic church says about demons is true, or "proof," at least, that spirits walk among us. In orb form.

The orb people are actually pretty tame compared to the *real* weirdos in the business. These particular weirdos always make for an interesting talking head on documentaries, so they're on TV enough that skeptical people can pretty easily get the idea that all ghost hunters are a bunch of kooks.

But they aren't. Troy Taylor has a few theories that I think are a bit out there, but he's actually quite skeptical about ghosts. He's also respectable enough that the town he lives in gave him the keys to the cemetery so that he could take tour groups in there after midnight. *That*, my friends, is serious trust. And the kooks in the scene give him no end of crap for being skeptical.

Troy Taylor was my boss in Chicago Spooks, and he became my partner in Weird Chicago. By then, he'd written dozens of books on ghosts and hauntings. One of his books, *The Ghost Hunter's Guidebook*, is probably the best book on the subject—members of The Atlantic Paranormal Society (TAPS), who starred on the *Ghost Hunters* TV show, used it to train new members of their team.

Troy describes himself as "skeptically optimistic" when it comes to ghosts. He's been to just about every famous haunted location you can name, but has only actually claimed to have seen a ghost himself once or twice. In person, Troy is pleasant and down to earth, no more New Agey than I am. He's maybe a little more prone to believing ghost stories than I am, but he's quite good about separating fact from fiction.

"Has Hector ever told you about that ghost without a face that he saw one time?" I asked him once.

He grinned. "I think Hector knows that if he told me a story like that, I'd laugh at him," he said.

As a well-known figure in the ghost business, Troy certainly does meet the weirdos. He hears from people who claim to live in haunted houses on a regular basis, and, while many of them are levelheaded people with legitimate stories, an awful lot of the people are pretty clearly nuts. Occasionally he forwards letters to me, including cases that the TAPS team passes on to him. A great many of them—perhaps even the majority—are from people who experience a couple of strange things, like doors opening by themselves around the house. Rather than looking into explanations like whether the door is hanging crooked or even whether there is psychokinetic activity, these individuals just jump straight to assuming that their house has been possessed by demons. The word "Satan" comes up in about half of the letters.

Every profession has people that are hard to deal with. When you work at Starbucks, you have to deal with people who want a decaf triple grande, nonfat, two-pumps-of-hazelnut, three-raw-sugar, no-foam, 180-degree latte and who will give you hell if the thing is only 175 degrees. Stockbrokers get people who think they've developed a code to beat the market based on the number of hairs on their butt. And ghost hunters get weirdos who think Satan has nothing better to do than open and close the doors in their house.

On tours that Troy runs, he's frequently approached by people wanting to show him pictures that appear to be nothing more than a picture of some leaves but that, they insist, show the ghost of Napoleon riding a horse if you look closely enough. (When we run tours together, Troy somewhat shamelessly "allows" me to handle these people.) A lot of "ghost evidence" requires you to look awfully, awfully closely and use your imagination.

With as much of this as he has to deal with, it's a wonder that Troy hasn't given up on the whole idea of ghosts, but he keeps on keeping on. As a part of my quest to figure out what the heck was going on in the world, ghost-wise, I sat down to talk with him at one of Chicago's haunted restaurants. We chatted about the tour business and swapped "difficult customer horror stories" for a bit, then turned the conversation to ghosts. Honestly, we had rarely spoken about them. We usually just talked about tour stuff and research.

"I always say that I believe in ghosts, but I don't believe everything I hear," he said. I've stolen this answer many times when the old "Do you believe in ghosts?" question comes up.

"I am always open to the *possibility* that a place might be haunted," Troy explained, "but that doesn't necessarily mean that it is. People come to me with stories of their personal hauntings all the time. In most cases, when I have checked out the stories they tell me, at the locations that they claim are haunted, I find there are simply natural explanations for the phenomenon they believe is supernatural."

"But you keep on looking?" I asked. "Don't you get discouraged?"

"My belief comes from personal experiences," he said. "I've been in many situations where events occurred that remain unexplainable. Were they ghosts? I don't know, but there was one occasion when I saw a ghost that couldn't be anything other than a full-blown apparition."

Here, Troy's voice began to take on a rhythm all its own—the guy's a born storyteller.

"I was in an abandoned hospital," he said, "that was reportedly haunted. And I saw a man—who looked solid and real—walk across the hallway about twenty-five feet ahead of me. He walked from one side to the other and entered a room on the opposite side from where he started. When I walked to the doorway to see who he was and what he was doing, I found the room was empty. There was no other exit but the man had simply disappeared. I would challenge anyone who states that they do not believe in ghosts to explain that. I was not drunk, hallucinating, or imagining things, and yet, it happened."

He went on to explain that what he looks for on a ghost investigation differs depending on *why* he's doing the investigation. If he's going through someone's house, he looks for crooked doorways, creaky floorboards, and the like to see if the reported hauntings can be explained away.

If he's working on a book or a story for a tour, that sort of thing isn't quite as necessary—all you need for that is the stories that people tell. When it goes in the book, the phrase "according to legend" takes over.

I smiled at this. I'd told plenty of stories on the tours that I had my doubts about just on the grounds that they were good stories, but I preferred to flag the ones I doubted—people who listened carefully on my tours would notice that I used the terms "apparently," "supposedly," "according to some reports," and "some people say" quite a lot.

But those are for the ghost stories. You still need the history to be reasonably solid.

"In my opinion," Troy said, "no authentic haunting can exist without the history to back it up. It's the events of the past that create the hauntings we experience today, so history is the essential piece of the puzzle."

To me, history is the main piece of the puzzle. If a few restaurant employees see a ghost and we can find some historical event to back it up, there's no way I can really tell them flat out that it *isn't* haunted. That doesn't mean there's really a ghost there, but if you have sightings and a verifiable story, well … plenty of places in Chicago are claiming to be haunted based on a lot less than that. If there's not a story behind the sightings, it's a lot easier for me to brush the place off.

"So," I asked, "what are we looking for when we look for ghosts? If science explains some way that an apparition can show up, does it still count as a ghost?"

"'Ghost' is a very generic term for a lot of different things," Troy said. "We all use it a lot, but honestly, 'spirits' and 'apparitions' are two very different things. I believe—and this is just my opinion—that a 'spirit' is a traditional type of ghost in that it's the personality of a person who once lived and at the time of death did not pass on to the other side. An 'apparition' is more like a recording. It's a moment of time that is imprinted on the atmosphere of a location, and it replays itself over and over again. I started calling these 'residual hauntings' back in the early nineteen nineties, and the term caught on. Anyway, these types of ghosts don't interact with anyone, because they are merely a bit of memory that has been left behind."

"But do those count as ghosts?" I asked. "Or will they continue to, if we ever really explain them away scientifically?"

"Sure," said Troy. "It's a generic term, but a ghost is a ghost."

Troy also had the best explanation I'd ever heard for whether it's actually possible to prove a haunting.

"Actually being able to 'prove' a haunting is 'real' scientifically is almost impossible," he said. "To do that, we have to force ghosts to perform on command in a laboratory, and that's never going to happen. However, many ghost researchers have been able to prove that houses are haunted—not scientifically, but historically."

"So, how does that work?" I asked.

"Well," said Troy, "say a family moves into a house and, shortly after, they begin to experience strange happenings. Doors open and close by themselves, lights turn on and off, and objects begin to vanish, turning up again in odd places a few days later. They are also startled to find that the apparition of a man is sometimes seen in an upstairs bedroom. So, they contact the previous owners of the property ..."

"And ask for their money back," I said.

"Well, maybe eventually," he said, "but first, they learn that the previous owners also experienced the odd happenings and saw the ghostly man. Checking back even further, they discover that other prior owners had shared these same experiences. Before this, none of them were aware that others had seen the same things. So, scientifically speaking, no one had proven that a ghost was haunting this house, but there is historical evidence of this fact."

"So that's proof?" I asked, as he sipped his drink.

"I believe that history in this case proved that the house was haunted," said Troy. "We can collect historical evidence by gathering witness testimony and details about the ghost that may be present at a location. We can then research the gathered information and match it to the former occupants of the house when they were still among the living. Even better, we may also be able to compare the current witness testimony with that of those who lived in the house before. This is all a bit simplified here, but having independent witnesses, of different time periods, with matching experiences, makes for some pretty compelling—and convincing—evidence."

"Well," I said, "it can prove that there's something weird in the house, but is it someone's soul, a bit of visual memory, or what?"

Troy shrugged. "That part is for the scientists to figure out," he said. "It's a ghost, whatever it is."

Once again, it all comes down to semantics.

I suppose that, by that logic, I've proven a few places were haunted myself, just by the historical research—including the one we were eating at right then.

Several employees of the restaurant had described seeing the ghost of a woman wearing a nightgown in the place. Through a whole heck of a lot of research, I was able to find out that a woman had been murdered in the place in the late 1890s, roughly the time period witnesses said the ghost seemed to come from, by a jealous lover who had then killed himself. The murder took place late at night, so she was likely to have been wearing a nightgown.

The obvious conclusion for a skeptic would be that the employees had heard the story and made up the ghost, but that's pretty unlikely—the history of that building was really tough to trace. The street name had changed a couple of times, the precise address of the building seemed to change with the whims of the owner, and the low-down saloons and mob-owned strip clubs wouldn't have kept very good records. Indeed, when I finally found the story of the murder-suicide, it was only a casual mention of a story that had been so well covered up that none of the neighbors even knew about it, and ascertaining which building the article was talking about took a lot of extra work, since the article wasn't very specific.

And, after hours of research, I hadn't found that part out myself when I first met with the management to go over my findings. Had they known of a murder-suicide in the 1890s, they probably would have led me on a bit or seemed disappointed that I hadn't found that out already. The story pretty well legitimized the haunting—after all, they had sightings *and* a story to explain it, something that a lot of famously haunted places in the city distinctly lack.

So there you have it.

I'm a skeptic, but I've proven a place was haunted. Exactly *what* is haunting the place is another matter, but it's haunted, all right.

Most of the work on the more serious investigations we did—the ones at the places where we thought there was genuine reason to think the reports of hauntings were caused by a ghost, not just a doorway hanging crooked—was actually done off-site in libraries, particularly after Troy, Ken, and I went into business for ourselves. We'd done research when we worked for the other company of course, but we really kicked it into high gear once we were working for ourselves.

I spent hours putting my English degree to work (believe it or not), doing research into the history of the locations and their inhabitants. I'd do only a little bit of research before going to a place for the first time—getting just the basics, so as not to color my imagination too much—and, if a place seemed to be worthy of it, I'd do a whole lot more. I pored over microfilm until my eyeballs felt like they were going to fall off before springing for the pay-per-search online archives, which are *much* easier to search. Even when there didn't turn out to be much information about a building, browsing through old newspapers is a lot of fun—they were really into advertising corsets and constipation cures back in the day, which are always funny to read, and I stumbled across some fantastic stories that hadn't been collected in any books of Chicago history before.

Sometimes this can end up being tricky detective work. For instance, H. H. Holmes, the serial killer who built a "murder castle" full of trapdoors, gas chambers, and any number of freaky stuff on the South Side in the 1890s, owned buildings all over the city under various aliases. How many people he actually killed will never be known. He confessed to twenty-seven murders, but Holmes was, in addition to his other unpleasant qualities, a chronic liar. A few of the people he claimed to have killed were actually still alive at the time, including one Kate Durkee, who told newspapers that she had "never been killed by Holmes or anyone else."

Since he had so many aliases and told so many lies, tracing Holmes's footsteps around Chicago has been quite a task. For example, one of his victims was a girl named Emily Van Tassel, a seventeen-year-old beauty who lived on Robey Street. Most books say she worked for Holmes as a secretary at the murder castle. Some come a little closer to the truth and say that she worked at the candy store in the murder castle. But when the story first broke, all of the newspapers said that she worked at Frank Wilde's Fruit and Candy Shop on Milwaukee Avenue, near Robey Street (which is now called Damen) on the other side of town from the castle.

Finding information about Frank Wilde's store was very tricky—the newspapers gave two different addresses, 1151 and 1152, for the shop. Those two would have been on opposite sides of the street. Luckily, we were able to ascertain from a 1909 street renumbering guide that, at least as of 1908, there was no building at 1152. Old maps pretty well confirmed that this was the case in 1893, as well.

But this brought up even more questions. We'd figured out where the shop was, but who was Frank Wilde? No information about Wilde has ever been found in census reports, but the 1890 census, the one we'd really need, burned up in a fire in the 1920s, leaving only fragments available to researchers.

Eventually, we found enough information to be reasonably certain that there was no Frank Wilde—it was just one of Holmes's aliases. He was, in fact, the owner of the candy store were Van Tassel worked. This gave us a whole new place we could bring the tours to that no other ghost or crime tour knew about. Better yet, we found that he most likely killed her at a glass-bending factory that he owned four blocks north—a spot that just happened (by sheer dumb luck) to be right between two regular Weird Chicago tour stops.

However, our research has shown us that most ghost stories have little or no basis in fact—often, people think they see a ghostly figure and make up a legend to explain it, and the legend catches on. There are lots and lots of train tracks where the ghosts of children killed in train or bus wrecks long ago are said to push cars across, but a number of these wrecks (the vast majority, in fact) never actually happened.[17] Similarly, there are a lot of good ghost stories going around about the ghosts of people who never really existed.[18]

Still, sometimes the background stories do turn out to be true. Sometimes the truth turns out to be even stranger than the legend. For instance, when I was told that we

---

17. The most famous version of this story is a variation in San Antonio. Around the tracks in question, the streets all have names of children who were supposedly killed in a bus accident on the tracks. The ghosts of these children now push stalled cars across the tracks, leaving their fingerprints on the cars. In fact, there was never any such accident anywhere near those tracks.

18. A good Chicago example is the ghost of Inez Clark, who is said to haunt Graceland Cemetery. In the cemetery is a statue of a young girl encased in glass, said to be the statue of young Inez, whose parents commissioned the statue after she was killed by a bolt of lightning. The story goes that Inez's ghost has been seen playing around the statue or that the statue has been known to vanish during storms. The problem is that Inez Clark never existed—the statue was built not as a gravestone but as an advertisement for a gravestone carver, and the only person buried beneath it is a boy named Amos. When this story hit the Chicago papers in 2007, they blamed Olga Durlochen of Chicago Spooks for making it up, though in fact she was probably just repeating an old story that had been going around for a while.

were going to investigate a local bar/apartment where, according to the owners, there had been an axe murder years before, I scoffed. This was Chicago—who owns an axe to begin with? It's not like apartment dwellers have a lot of forestry to chop down.

But the story turned out to be not even the half of it—the location had been the site of *two* axe murders, thirty years apart, with a pop-bottle bludgeoning in the middle. At the time of the bludgeoning, the place had been a transient men's shelter in which two men—a twenty-eight-year-old and a seventy-year-old—got into an argument over a pair of pants. Now, these were probably not fancy designer pants; they were just the kind of dirty, urine-soaked pants that you would expect to find on the floor of a transient men's shelter. Still, the twenty-eight-year-old decided he'd kill for such a pair of pants. He beat the old man over the head with a pop bottle, then kicked him out of the window. No one was sure if the old man died from the fall or if he was already dead when he landed, but, in any case, he was dead, and the story was verifiable with a quick search of the newspaper archives.

But it was rare that things were this cut and dry. Sometimes it took a lot more digging, and the more digging I did, the more complicated it became to find out the truth about a place. With many of the more historical cases, no two books or articles really agreed on many of the details. Even accounts from witnesses of the Iroquois Theater fire and the *Eastland* disaster differed wildly.

For instance, take the ghost of Nellie Reed. Nellie was the only performer who was killed in the Iroquois Theater fire (or one of only two or only three, depending on which source you believe). People who work backstage at the Oriental Theatre on Randolph Street—which was built over the foundation of the old Iroquois Theater—have occasionally reported seeing the ghost of a woman wearing a tutu. A silhouette of a woman in a tutu has also been seen along the wall in the haunted alley behind the theater. It's to be assumed that it's the ghost of Nellie Reed, a trapeze artist in the show, on the grounds that no one else in their right mind would have been wearing a tutu in Chicago on December 30, the day of the fire.

But exactly how she died is a bit unclear. One source says that when the fire broke out, she was on her platform, preparing to swing out above the audience and drop flowers on their heads, and she never made it down from the platform. Another says that she was suspended from a wire over the stage and was left hanging in the midst of the fire. Still another says that she wasn't onstage at all, but in an upstairs dressing room. Everyone else in the dressing rooms escaped by taking the elevator, but Nellie tried to run down the burning staircase instead, due to a fear of elevators—a phobia that didn't exactly pay off. Quite a few accounts say that she actually escaped, badly burned, into the alley behind the theater, only to die in the hospital hours later. The *Chicago Tribune* alone has published three or four wildly different accounts of her death over the years.

This is pretty much par for the course, as far as documenting the stories is concerned. No one really knows, for instance, who the shooters at the Saint Valentine's Day Massacre were—there's a new theory presented as fact about every six months or so, but we'll never know for sure. No one can agree on whether John Dillinger was armed when he was shot down in the alley outside of the Biograph Theater—indeed, plenty of people (Troy, for one) are certain that it wasn't even actually Dillinger who was shot, but a lookalike fall guy named Jimmy Lawrence.

We'll never know the truth about this stuff. Not really.

And this is just the historical stuff—the easy part. Actually tracking down a firsthand source for the ghost stories themselves can be practically impossible. Indeed, I found out early on that a lot of the most famous Chicago ghost stories were probably just made up by other ghost tour guides over the years as excuses to go to some historical location or another. In some cases, those tour guides are the only people ever to have seen a certain ghost.

Of course, it's a pretty hard-and-fast rule of tour guides (ghost or otherwise) never to let facts get in the way of a good story. After all, people don't come on ghost tours to learn about science, they come for thrills and chills and to have a good time. Troy himself said that the tours, and even the books, were mostly just for entertainment—scientific research was something else altogether. As worried as I was about getting the stories right, and as hard as I tried to appear credible and levelheaded, I found that most people assumed I was making up most of the stories any-way. When we ran into people who worked in the theater in Death Alley who told us about ghosts that they'd seen, people assumed they were on our payroll (ha!).

For a while, telling stories that I doubted gave me some-thing of a moral dilemma, but I eventually decided that, as long as I flagged the ones I couldn't verify with endless varia-tions on the phrase "according to legend," it didn't matter much. These were ghost stories, after all. Whether or not they happen to be true has no impact on their effect on culture.

Meanwhile, Back at the Tattoo Shop

No one knows how many ghosts there are supposed to be in Chicago, and there's no way that anyone can come up with a complete list. We can come up with a good list of *well-known* ghosts, but the number of buildings around the city that are thought to be haunted by the people who live and work inside them is pretty much endless. Honestly, it's hard to find an old building that *isn't* supposed to be haunted.

On North Clark Street, near the river, there was a bit of a dead zone in the space between Bughouse Square and the site of the *Eastland* disaster where there wasn't much to talk about on my original Chicago Spooks route. So, to kill time, Hector and I made up a ghost story about the adult bookstore we drove past. As it always was with the stories I made up, it wasn't a ghost story so much as a joke—when I was making up a story outright, I wanted people to be able to tell. Hector and I sort of refined the joke together over a few weeks, adding a bit to it every night until it became a really complicated story.

"If you look to your right," I'd say, "You'll see the haunted adult bookstore. We do *lots* of investigations at the haunted adult bookstore."

"Hell yeah!" Hector said, while people chuckled.

"The story goes," I said, "that the place was originally opened by a woman who was a fairly famous stripper several decades ago. But then she lost her leg in a shuffleboard accident, and her leg was sold to P. T. Barnum, who put it on display in a vat of formaldehyde as part of his sideshow. Within a year, her leg was making more money than she was. So she quit stripping and started up this store, then spent years writing letter after letter to P. T. Barnum, asking if he'd sell her her leg back."

"Is this true?" someone would usually ask.

"Of course it is," I say, making it fairly obvious that I was lying.

"Tell them about the footsteps," Hector would say.

"I'm about to," I'd say. "You see, after she died, they started hearing mysterious footsteps all over the building. Or, well, foot *step* anyway."

I'd tap on the microphone to mimic a single footstep, and people would start to groan. But the joke wasn't over. Hector provided the punchline.

"On the day she died," Hector said, "they finally got a letter back from Barnum. It said, 'Honey, if you want that thing back, it's gonna cost you an arm and a leg!'"

"Good night, folks!" I'd say.

"Try the veal!" Hector would add, and we'd do a little dance.

By the time we got that far, I'd be at the site of the *Eastland*, ready to get back to telling *real* stories of death and tragedy.

I always felt like it was fairly obvious that that story was just a joke, but a few people e-mailed and told me that they'd gone to the place after the tour to look for the ghost.

Nearly two years after I first told the story, Ken started running a red-light district tour for Weird Chicago—a tour that took people to a couple of old brothel sites (and a couple of current ones). That very adult bookstore was a regular stop. One night, when I was riding along on that tour, I introduced myself to the owner.

"I just wanted to apologize," I said, "in case anyone ever came in asking about the ghost of a one-legged stripper."

I explained the story to him, and he seemed amused.

"That happens now and then," he said, "and we always thought it was weird, because, the thing is, we really *do* have a ghost here!"

And this wasn't the only time this happened. Troy once ran a pub crawl where he was offered a hundred bucks to add an extra stop at the end of the route. Because everyone was too drunk to care about the story, he quickly made up a ghost story about the nearest pub. It turned out that the staff of that place had actually thought it was haunted for years.

We looked into the history of all of these places, and some of them turned out to have really good stories behind them. But even the spookiest places didn't always have a *very* good story. Like Odin Tatu, for instance. Sure, it was a funeral parlor, but who the heck dies in a funeral parlor?

Well, besides Tapeworm, that is.

When Tapeworm died, Hector and I speculated that maybe, on some level, he had known that he didn't have much time left when we did our first investigation. Ever since I was a kid, I've always sort of suspected that sometimes, before people die, they know in the back of their minds that their time is short, even if the death is completely unexpected. This is one of those beliefs (or suspicions, rather) that's stuck with me even as I've grown more skeptical.

Right after Tapeworm's death, Hector and I began to talk about him on the tours, filling in the space between Harpo Studios and Hull House. And we speculated that, since he *had* challenged the ghosts to a fight in the event of his death, that he was now engaged in a battle royale

(*Immortal Kombat*, if you will) with the ghost of Walter, the ghost who had said his name into the microphone. And, even if Walter had picked up some really crafty tricks in the afterlife during the years in which he'd been dead, my money was still on Tapeworm.

But we didn't make a return trip to Odin Tatu for some time. Even after they reopened for business, we didn't want to impose—there's really no Miss Manners guide to etiquette out there to tell you how long to wait after someone dies before you can ask his friends if you can come see if his ghost is up and around (though I suspect that the answer is "never").

Finally, one wintry day they called Ken and asked if we'd like to come check the place out again. We dropped everything and headed up, planning to record an episode of our Weird Chicago podcast during the impromptu investigation.

Except for the fact that the tattoo people no longer rented, or had access to, the upstairs apartment area where Tapeworm had lived, the place was pretty much the same as it had been before. The gravestone was still in the fireplace. Lots of the Star Wars memorabilia was still around. Tapeworm's station in the tattoo parlor, where he had done his work, was still there, untouched and unused. They left it up as sort of a shrine.

"Has anything weird been happening here?" we asked the people—friends of Tapeworm's—who now ran the place.

"A couple of people have heard the little girl," said one of them. "Chango, you heard it, right? Come here!"

A guy got up from his station and walked toward the back.

"Chango?" asked Ken. "There's a guy here named Chango?"

Shortly after they'd reopened, they had hired a new tattoo artist who was nicknamed Chango—the name of the orisha of whom Tapeworm had been so fond and also Tapeworm's own boyhood nickname.

"Yeah," said Chango. "I was in the back room, and I heard this faint sound coming from out in the entryway, like a little girl crying. And I came out to see what it was, and there was nobody out here."

They also told us about flickering lights and of glass display shelves that were falling apart inside of their cases. Lots of people had been "feeling" the presence of the little girl. One person had even seen her—a little blonde girl, peeking around the corners. No one was totally sure that the girl that people heard and the girl that people saw were one and the same, of course. We never can be sure of these things. They could be ghosts of two different girls or possibly even two separate ghosts of the same person, for all we know. That sort of thing has been known to happen.

We proceeded into the basement, which was spookier than ever. The lighting had been removed from the place, so I was walking around, taking photograph after photograph, not so much to hunt for ghosts—I wasn't even looking through the viewfinder—but to use the flash as a flashlight.

Unlike the first time—when we got nothing unusual in the photographs—we were at least picking up some orbs this time. But they were, without question, just dust particles. It was awfully dusty down there.

There was, however, one strange thing that happened: Every time I took a photograph, I'd see two silhouettes on the back wall of the basement. One, of course, was Ken. The other was of Nick, one of the tattoo guys. Neither silhouette was showing up in the pictures, though.

One time, only once, there was a third silhouette. I only saw it for a split second, but I was absolutely sure that it was Tapeworm.

It could have just been my mind playing tricks on me. But it was a sighting of a ghost made not from photos or audio recordings, but with my own two eyes. That's incredibly rare.

That split-second sighting was all that happened that was out of the ordinary that night. The next day, though, we got an e-mail from Keegan, one of the young psychics who had been on the first investigation.

"In my dream last night," she wrote, "we were in Odin Tatu, all of us, and you were doing an investigation and while you were doing it, Tapeworm and I were watching. Then I went to say hi to you, and he told me not to, since I would be interrupting." The dream had been so vivid that she felt she had to write to see if we were okay. She had no idea that we had been there that night. In fact, at the time of our investigation, she was most likely asleep.

As the months went by, we got occasional reports back from the tattoo parlor that a lot of weird stuff was going on. Over the summer, about a year after Tapeworm died, they installed some motion-sensor cameras that were picking up weird, orblike blobs. My first instinct was to say that they were dust particles, but they weren't *behaving* like dust. They were larger than dust particles, for one thing. And dust alone shouldn't have set off the motion sensor. And the way that they moved wasn't really consistent with what we'd see from dust—dust particles don't normally float up to the camera, pause in front of it, and then float away. Many of them seemed to be moving with a sense of purpose.

On Halloween night, during a party in the tattoo parlor, one of the employees noticed that he'd missed a call on his cell phone. No message was left, and it turned out that the number belonged to a random woman who was apparently asleep at the time the call was made. But the employee recognized the number—it used to belong to Tapeworm.

Normally, I would say that you're not really much more likely to see ghosts on Halloween; they get reported all year. But knowing Tapeworm, I would have expected him to be a bit more active that night. It's just the kind of guy he was.

In the fall of 2007, about a year after Tapeworm's death, we started bringing tour groups to the parlor—we even managed to get permission to take tour groups down into the basement. One of the benefits of having a smaller bus than we'd used for Chicago Spooks was that we could get our groups into places that couldn't really handle large crowds.

Like any place, it was more active some nights than others. Some nights we'd go down there, and it wouldn't even seem all that spooky. Other nights, though, it was terrifying. Cold spots were recorded frequently. On a couple of occasions, we smelled a strong aroma of formaldehyde for a couple of minutes that disappeared as mysteriously as it had appeared. Another night, there was a smell that people described as "the smell of decay." On many of the more active nights, I would feel like someone was tapping my shoulder, flicking my hair, and tweaking single hairs off of my head—all of the annoying things that guys like Tapeworm do to nerds like me.

Soon, I was telling people that I was a skeptic, but if there was ever a ghost that I believed in, it was the ghost of Tapeworm. I don't bother myself with questions over whether ghosts are proof of the afterlife or if "being" a ghost is a form of the afterlife, but Tapeworm is in that building all right. If I screw my skepticism to the sticking place, I can go so far as to say that he's still there in our hearts, that his spirit hangs over the place the way the spirit of the Beatles infests the Cavern Club.

But, one way or the other, he's still there all right.

The Ghosts Check In...

One afternoon, Ken and I were standing with a group of tourists in the Gold Room, the largest ballroom of the Congress Hotel. We were in hour four of a six-hour "crime tour" that we were conducting on a cold winter's day. Crime tours generally don't get too into ghost stories, but we still throw in a few.

"Now, one of the ghost stories here at the hotel is of a guy named Captain Louis Ostheim," I said. "Being named Captain Lou is enough to make him one of my five or six favorite ghosts in town all by itself, but his story is really sad; he was the first person to die here of anything other than natural causes, as far as we know. He was freshly back from serving in the Spanish-American War and staying in the hotel, where he was known to be suffering from night terrors—really bad nightmares. One night, in the middle of what was apparently a really bad one, he woke up and shot himself in the head. Just to make it even more tragic, he was supposed to be married the next day."

"You know, Adam," Ken said. "I just thought of something. Do you happen to know what room Ostheim was in?"

"Not off the top of my head," I said.

"Because I wonder if he might be the shadow figure ghost," said Ken. "The one that scared the marines. He's associated with nightmares and the military, right?"

I nodded. On our first investigation of the place, the staff had told us that a group of four marines had run out of their room in the middle of the night after one woke up to see a shadowy figure at the foot of his bed. His screams woke up the others, and the shadowy figure was frightening enough to them that they all ran—not quite dressed—to the lobby, refusing to go back to their room.

"What floor were they on?" Ken asked the security guard who was accompanying us.

"Seven south," she said. "They were all in their skivvies when they came down."

"Well, I guess it wasn't Captain Lou, then," said Ken. "The south wing wasn't built yet when Captain Lou died."

"So what?" I asked. "If the guy can come back from the dead, I'm sure he can walk down a hall!"

Everyone had a good chuckle, of course, but we refrained from asking the big question that this invited: how mobile are ghosts? Can they wander around or are they restricted to a certain locale? Getting into that could have taken up the remainder of the six-hour tour.

Going back to the hypothesis that ghosts are real to begin with, the answer, as usual, varies from ghost to ghost. Some seem to haunt only the exact spot where they died. Others haunt the area within a few feet of the spot. Still others seem to have the run of the entire building or grounds on which they died or, occasionally, the place where they hung out when they were alive. Others are even more mobile, appearing in whole different continents at various times. There are examples of all of these—and more—among the ghosts said to haunt the Congress Hotel.

More than a century old, the place is full of nooks, crannies, passageways, and spooky stories. It was built in 1893 to accommodate the tourists who came to Chicago for the World's Fair that was held that year. At the time, it was a five-star hotel, as modern as anything anyone could imagine.

The years haven't been totally kind to the hotel; some of the renovations designed to modernize it over the years didn't help much. Replacing the orchestras with radios, for instance. In the 1930s, Benny Goodman and Duke Ellington both played long stands in the hotel ballrooms. Replacing Benny Goodman with a radio may have seemed modern at the time, but it sure doesn't seem like progress to me.

It was moves like this—made by hotels all over the city—that ended the era when hotels were *the* places to hang out. Looking at parts of the hotel are like looking at an old movie star today—you can see every wrinkle and the spring is gone from its step, but you can still see the glamour beneath the surface. The hotel is practically a ghost itself.

Isn't this the very essence of why some of us want ghosts to be real? So we can believe that the bits of the past that we treasure aren't really gone? Are the old-fashioned ballrooms serving the exact same function as an actual ghost? Well, let's not get bogged down in semantics. Not this time anyway.

That the Congress is haunted (by the spooky kind of ghosts, not just the old reminders of the past that still hang in the walls and gather dust in the basement) is sort of a given around the city. Hotels are not as frequently thought to be haunted as, say, abandoned mental hospitals or prisons, but old hotels are right up there on the list of "types of places that always seem to be haunted."

We first investigated the place in early summer of 2006, just a couple of weeks before the Odin Tatu investigation. Ken and Olga were running a public investigation with a group of people who had signed up to come along, and Hector and I both assisted.

I did a bit of research early on, but felt as though I'd barely scratched the surface. There were a lot of stories about the Congress on the Internet that seemed like utter nonsense—including a classic Chicago myth: "Al Capone used to own it." Capone probably spent some time there, but he certainly never owned the place or lived there.

The ghosts said to haunt it included Frank Lloyd Wright, Thomas Edison, and Franklin D. Roosevelt, all of whom stayed there at one point or another. This made me a bit nervous. My first book, which was about to be published at the time of the first investigation, threw a few comic insults in Edison's direction, and I supposed there was always a chance that his ghost was going to want to kick my ass. But I figured that the ghost, should he exist, probably didn't read every young-adult novel that came out, even if he could get them up there in the afterlife a few months before they're published down here. I certainly hoped not—Edison was the kind of guy who electrocuted elephants to prove points.

Another ghost listed as haunting the place was Theodore Roosevelt, who had quite a bit of history with the building. In 1912, Roosevelt, having returned from safari in Africa, decided to run for another term as president. He stayed in the Congress during the Republican convention that was held at the nearby Coliseum, where he was more or less robbed of the nomination by President Taft. Outraged, Roosevelt jumped on a table in the Florentine Room, one of the ballrooms, and said something along the lines of "Screw this, I'm outta here!" He was back in the same room six weeks later, setting up a headquarters to become the nominee of the Progressive Party, which would come to be known as the Bull Moose party.

I reasoned that if *anyone* could come back from the dead to wander down a hallway, it would be Teddy Roosevelt (I hadn't met Tapeworm yet). In fact, by this time I was willing to go along with the theory that people could leave behind a sort of emotional residue or psychic imprint on a place. Once again, I wouldn't say I *believed* it, exactly, but I *suspected* that something like that could happen. And, given Roosevelt's legendary energy, it's possible that the guy may have been like the Johnny Appleseed of psychic imprints, leaving little ghosts of himself behind wherever he went. As an EVP guy, picking up a mysterious voice saying "Bully!" would have been a regular Holy Grail (though, if it happens now that I've mentioned it, anyone with any sense will probably assume that I faked it).

However, none of the staff had ever heard of Edison or Roosevelt—or any of the other famous guys—haunting the place. And some of them had been working there for decades.

But the staff had some good ghost stories of their own.

One thing I'd seen in online reviews was that TVs in the hotel had a tendency to turn on and off by themselves—which we ghost hunters would call poltergeist activity. Some of the staff attributed this to the ghost of a guy known as the Judge. He was the last permanent resident of the hotel, a relic of the days when old people moved into hotels. In his declining years, the Judge's favorite way to have a good time was to scoot around in his wheelchair, using his remote control to turn peoples' TVs off and on from the hallway. I liked to imagine him wheeling slowly around with a goofy, satisfied smile on his face as he listened to the annoyed guests behind the doors trying to watch The A Team.

Others told us about a phantom piano in the Gold Room, the still-lovely old ballroom that looked like a scene from the Haunted Mansion at Disneyland. Photographs that we took when the lights were out in that room picked up *tons* of orbs—all dust particles, but pretty spooky-looking anyway.

The security guard who was escorting us told us about a phantom piano that showed up in pictures of the room from time to time.

"Now, you're the psychic," he said to Ken. "You tell me where the piano was."

Ken began to walk around, his arms outstretched, looking like he was concentrating. I started to panic—I'd never really seen him in action before. What if he was wrong? We'd all look rather stupid.

But Ken walked back over to the guard and pointed to a spot on the floor. "Right there, I think," said Ken. "I might be wrong, but I think it was right there."

"No, you're right," said the security guard. "That's right where it shows up."

I've seen a lot of psychics put to the test, but Ken is the only one who ever seems to pass.

Even spookier than the Gold Room was the Florentine Room, a smaller, hardwood-floored room with Italian-style paintings—not unlike the cover of most copies of *The Canterbury Tales*—all over the ceiling. It wasn't as large as the Gold Room, or as fancy, but the place had a weird vibe about it—that haunted vibe.

"This one's pretty spooky at night," said the guard. "I once had an old couple ask to see it because they wanted to see the room where they had their first date—this room was a skating rink years and years ago. And one night, I heard music coming from it."

"What kind of music?" I asked.

"Calliope-type music," said the guy. "The kind they played at skating rinks back then, I guess."

He then told us that there had been phantom dancers seen around the room, dancing back and forth, and that several people had reported feeling a hand on their shoulder in that particular room. Several other guards ended up backing him up on that one.

At one point, I went upstairs to the room Olga had rented for the night—a twelfth-floor room where a woman had died in the 1970s. I had left an audio recorder running in it (the recording later revealed that the phone had been ringing off the hook while we were out of the room, for some reason), and I went up to change the discs. When I stepped out of the room, I suddenly became overwhelmed with the feeling that someone was right behind me, and I took off running. I ran like hell, like a total chicken, down the hall and into the waiting elevator. I wouldn't have looked back behind me for anything—it's all very well and good to be a skeptic and everything, but in the middle of a haunted hallway, you can still chicken out sometimes.

It was only after that that I heard about the ghost of the little boy in the hotel. The little boy was seen—sometimes just standing around, but usually running back and forth—all over the building, but most commonly on the twelfth floor, where I'd just been chased.

Maybe I'd missed my chance to actually see an apparition. Or maybe I was just being a wuss. Probably the latter.

Other people on the staff had more stories for us. A couple repeated a legend that some guy had been murdered by being walled up somewhere inside the building—a story that seems to be total fiction.

Others—quite a few others—told us that lately they'd been getting calls from the seventh floor of the south wing from guests saying that there was a vagrant with (get this) a peg leg lying around in the hall. And not a modern prosthetic leg, either—a regular Long John Silver type of peg leg.

Lesson number one: tell a bunch of ghost hunters that there's a ghost with a peg leg on the seventh floor, and they will make a beeline to that very floor. In fact, there may very well end up being a ghost-hunters-shaped hole left in the nearest wall after they charge through, cartoon-style, in their hurry to get there. We looked that floor up and down for any sign of Peg Leg Johnny, but, alas, came up empty-handed. However, a few weeks later, someone from the group found a news item stating that a hobo with a peg leg had been murdered in the hotel decades ago.

The best thing we found on that investigation wasn't particularly ghostly—it was just a bit of plaster sticking out of a wall and wrapping around a bit of crossbar in a closet near the Gold Room. It was too far back behind a bunch of junk for us to get close to it, but we cracked a few jokes about it looking like a hand—perhaps that of the guy who had been walled-up—grabbing the crossbar, and we took a picture or two. Then, when we blew the picture up, damned if there wasn't four fingers and a thumb on the thing. Perhaps it was a glove that got plastered over, some construction worker's idea of a joke. Or perhaps it really was Drywall Dave, reaching out for freedom and grabbing on to the crossbar. Or, going even further out on a limb, it could have been Teddy Roosevelt, carrying a big stick.

Back in the hotel room, we talked about what we'd seen and found. No one felt as though they'd seen a ghost or even been creeped out, except for me. My being chased down the hall was the best story we had.

I changed the discs out again, but kept recording.

"Are we going to ask some questions?" asked Olga.

"Like, to ghosts?" asked Ken. "Adam and I usually feel kind of stupid doing that."

"Oh, come on, we've got to!" said Olga.

Ken and I shrugged our shoulders and sat down in a circle with the rest of the group. I had everyone say their name, so that if I picked up any strange voices, I could figure out if it was just someone from the group.

We knew that a woman had died in the room in which we were sitting—but we didn't know who it was or what had happened. Some said it was a suicide, others pointed to an accidental death in the bathroom. You can only ask so many questions when you don't really know who you're talking to.

Ken started with our usual "first question," the good old "Do you need help with anything?" But there was no response. He paused for a minute, then asked, "Is one of your favorite bands Big Brother and the Holding Company?"

I thought I heard a noise in the room at that point, but nothing came up on the recording. I did find out later that that band had played in the auditorium across the street—odds are good that they stayed in the hotel, which was connected to the auditorium via a tunnel.

We went around asking whatever questions came to mind. After a few minutes, what Ken calls my "deep inner need to be a smart-ass" took over, and I asked the ghost if it ever spied on people in the shower.

"Come on!" said Hector. "Who do you think this ghost is? Moaning Myrtle from Harry Potter?"

A minute later, getting back in a properly spooky mode, Ken asked a question about the other ghosts in the hotel. When I played back the recording later, it was there that I picked up a voice—a vaguely female voice that sounded like it was saying, "That boy didn't know!"

I would never have claimed that piece of EVP as ghost evidence. It was the all-too-common kind of EVP that sounds like Charlie Brown's teacher—sort of mechanical and garbled. At the end of the investigation, all that we had was one garbled piece of EVP, some photographs of dust in the Gold Room that looked reasonably orbish, a picture of a weird hand, and my own feeling of being chased. Nothing that couldn't very easily be explained away.

But we sure got some good stories out of it. Enough to make me want to go back and explore some more—half of the fun of investigations, after all, is getting to poke around old buildings. It reminded me of being six years old and exploring my grandparents' apartment building with my cousins, riding around on the elevators and running down the hallways just for the heck of it.

In fact, about a year and a half later, Ken and I hit on the idea of taking tour groups to the hotel. It started as a stop on our tour based on the World's Fair of 1893 and the murderers associated with it. There wasn't much left from the fair to show people, so we hit on the idea of showing them the hotel, which was built to accommodate tourists who came to see the fair. When that went well, we decided to try it out as a ghost tour stop, and I threw myself head-first into researching the place. I tracked down newspaper stories detailing all sorts of deaths, murders, and suicides that took place in the hotel.

In the research, I came across a few possible deaths that may account for the ghostly little boy. The most likely theory dates to 1939. A Jewish family had fled Czechoslovakia when Hitler took over, and they had come to Chicago, but the persecution the family received at the hands of German immigrants in the city apparently drove the wife to madness. One day, shortly after arriving in Chicago, she checked into a room in the Congress Hotel—one on the floor that the boy runs up and down—and, in what was ruled a case of temporary insanity, she jumped from the window, taking her sons, six-year-old Karel and four-year-old Jan, with her. It's stories like this—which I run across a lot in this line of work—that can really make you think life sucks.

Stories about strange deaths and suicides in the place kept piling up: A slogan writer—coiner of the phrase "safety first"—who died in his room (of heart trouble; it would have been funnier if he had slipped in the shower or something). An opera singer who died just before he was supposed to go onstage across the street. Captain Lou certainly wasn't the only guy to shoot himself in his room; one guy offered the orchestra leader five hundred dollars to play "The Dead March," bought drinks for everyone in the ballroom until he was flat broke, then went to his room and shot himself. Quite a few people jumped from their windows.

Not all of the stories were bad, though. There was once a marble-lined tunnel known as Peacock Alley connecting the hotel to the Auditorium Theatre across the street. Everyone loves a good tunnel story. And, during a six-month stand in the Joseph Urban Room, Benny Goodman and his orchestra introduced most of the city to swing music—some musical historians actually credit that stand with redefining American popular music.

After a couple of tours that successfully featured the ballrooms of the Congress, Ken and I decided to make it a regular stop. To commemorate the occasion, we decided to do another investigation there, recording an episode for our podcast. Since the 2008 presidential primaries were heating up, I hit on the idea of saying we were picking up where the mainstream media left off. While they sought out senators and celebrities to see which candidate they endorsed, we would be the only "journalists" (another job I had crept into through the back door) to give Teddy Roosevelt's ghost a chance to endorse someone in time for Super Tuesday.

Of course, to get his opinion, we were going to have to get him to show up.

I've tried lots of things to get ghosts to show up. Talking to them usually only succeeds in making me feel like a dope, but sometimes it's worth a shot. Sometimes I've said, "Hello" or "Can I help you with anything?" Sometimes I've said, "What's your name?" Sometimes I've said, "I'm a talent scout for a major Hollywood studio. Can you please sing a few bars into the microphone?" Other times, it's "I'm going to the store. Anyone need anything?" It usually yields the same result: nothing. I figured that when Theodore Roosevelt declined the chance to shoot off his mouth right in the middle of one of our tours during which we recorded the podcast, it was pretty solid proof that Roosevelt wasn't haunting that room.

But, that same tour, someone took a picture of the wall while I was asking the questions, and the flash that reflected on the wall seemed to show an angry face of someone who, believe it or not, looked about like Theodore Roosevelt. Judging by the picture, Roosevelt was back, and he was pissed. Maybe he thought I was patronizing him. Or maybe it was a residual ghost left behind in that bitter June of 1912 when the nomination was stolen from him by his old best friend.

Of course, as a skeptic, I don't think it's really the ghost of Roosevelt showing up in the picture—our brains are trained to look for faces in random visual noise (we call this "matrixing"), and if I hadn't been talking about Roosevelt right then, it probably never would have occurred to me, or anyone else, to see his face in that picture.

But I do tend to get interested when we get photos with faces, particularly because some of them look pretty damned cool—especially the ones we get at the tattoo place. Orbs that appear to have faces in them are common enough, and easy enough to explain away, but there are two specific faces that seem to turn up over and over in that basement—one is Tapeworm, and the other is an old guy who looks kinda like the guy on the Quaker Oats box. I don't care how many ways those faces can be explained—they were terribly cool.

That was about the only "evidence" I found at the Congress in the first several months that we used it as a stop-off point, but we began to gather quite a collection of stories about ghosts there. It was quite a wide variety of spooks, just going by the variations in mobility—some of them seem to hang around all over the hotel, others were only ever seen in one room. Captain Lou has been pointed to as the ghost that scared the marines *and* as a guy dressed as a groom who shows up in the Gold Room. The little boy shows up more frequently in one hallway than anywhere else, but he turns up all over the place. Peg Leg Johnny even seems to be able to get around pretty well for a one-legged dead guy. Similarly, the fact that the Judge was in a wheelchair sure doesn't seem to be slowing him down.

Assuming that all of these are real ghosts, we can learn a lot from them, but what we learn would bring up a lot more questions about ghosts than it would answer.

The Ghosts Keep Coming

The ghost tour business, at least in Chicago, is not the kind of industry where competing companies get together to play softball every now and then. And it's unfortunate.

When we started Weird Chicago, our philosophy, as far as other tour companies were concerned, was to live and let live. This worked out well. We'd frequently run into Hector while he ran a Chicago Spooks tour, and we'd pull the buses alongside one another.

"What's up, man?" I'd ask. "Seeing anything good lately?"

"Oh, yeah," he said. "We got a video of the little girl at Hull House, man!"

"Sweet!" I'd say. "Send it along!"

I'd introduce him to my tour group, and he'd introduce me to his. Then, as he drove away, I'd explain that most of the ghost tour guides in the city knew each other and that we were all friends. We shared information and everything. People got a kick out of it. I got a kick out of it. Nothing warms my heart more than friendship between rivals.

But all of that fell apart after Hector was fired from Chicago Spooks. Exactly why Hector was fired, I never found out. But after that, Ray was both driving the bus and running most of the tours himself.

Since our buses picked up at the same place, people would occasionally ask him if they were in the right place for our tour. Sometimes he told them "I fired those guys!" Other times he'd start railing about how he "wrote" our tour. Other times, he'd tell people he'd never heard of us. Sometimes he'd even chew the people out for wanting to go on one of our tours.

On a couple of occasions, Ken would go out to the bus—which we parked in his neighborhood—and find that someone had spray-painted over the windshield and logos or bashed in the headlights. We had no way of knowing who was doing it, but we only ever had one suspect.

When we ran into Ray during tours, it was nothing like running into Hector had been. Usually he'd ignore us. One night Ken said hello to him, and Ray responded by saying, "Don't get cocky!"

The way Ken described it, this very nearly led to a boxing match. "Don't get cocky or *what*?" he asked Ray.

When Ray didn't respond, Ken challenged him further. "Come on!" he said. "I wanna know! Or *what*, Ray?"

I kept thinking that any night, I was going to run into Ray and his tour group in an alley someplace—Death Alley, presumably—and our respective tour groups would have a rumble. I imagined that it would be a lot like the "Beat It" video.

In the spring of 2008, I was walking toward the bank when I heard a voice shout "Adam!" It was Hector, driving by in a delivery truck he was driving at the time.

"Hector!" I shouted. I ran out into the street, and we shook hands and bitched about Ray for a while. I gave him an update on how things were going over at the tattoo parlor and the Congress, both of which he'd investigated with us, and both of which were now occasional tour stops for Weird Chicago.

"Hey, man," he said, "I need to get back into the scene. You guys ever need a driver or anything these days?"

"I'll let you know," I said.

And, a few weeks later, Willie's schedule changed, and we needed a new Friday night driver. Ken suggested Hector, and I was all for it. Hector agreed, and we had the whole old gang back together.

But he also said, "I'm not going to be the peanut gallery for you guys, though. I'll just be the driver, and that's it."

I knew, of course, that he wouldn't be sticking to this. Hector was never the sort who could resist even the smallest crowd.

The night of Hector's first tour back with me, we all met up at Ken's new house on the Northwest Side where

Hector

the bus was parked, and we showed Hector how we'd fixed up the bus into a sort of rolling museum of Chicago history. He'd only driven it once before, and that had been back before we'd even had it painted.

"Man," he said. "You know this is probably the first time we've all been in the same place in at least a year?"

It was true—the last time we'd met up was a night that I tagged along on one of Ken's tours, and we ran into Hector at the *Eastland* site. We hadn't all just hung out in months. But it felt right.

As we drove through the city to the pickup spot, Hector and I went through all of our old routines to see which jokes we could bring back and which ones we should just put to rest. We came up with some new ones. Hector had an idea for a new "character" he could play named Peanut, a very quiet, very stupid bus driver. He would barely open his mouth for the whole tour, except to say something stupid, then, midway through, whoever was running the tour would say, "Damn it, Peanut! How do you even tie your shoes in the morning? What job did you have before this?"

And "Peanut" would quietly say, "I was a tour guide for Chicago Spooks."

It was a perfect persona for nights that he worked with Ken, who didn't like sharing the stage as much as I did.

The tour that night, of course, was a blast. As I predicted, Hector was just as boisterous as ever. When we pulled up to the Hard Rock Cafe, they were blasting "Bohemian Rhapsody" over the speakers, and we headbanged so hard to the guitar solo that I was sore for days. Everyone was having a blast before the tour even began.

I hadn't been going to Hull House much, even though I'd found out some new information about it recently, but working with Hector made me want to swing by there again. Hector had told me that he'd had some interesting success looking for ghosts there with a pendulum. As a firm believer that you never know what kind of nutty gear might prove useful in a ghost hunt, I was eager to see it.

After telling the stories of the place and letting people out to look around, Hector pulled a crystal on a pendulum out of a pouch he was wearing around his neck and held it in front of him, staring at it intently.

"Pendulum," he said, "is there a ghost here?"

The pendulum moved a bit.

"Do you really have to address it like that?" I said.

"Yes," said Hector. "Pendulum, is there a ghost in the garden?"

The pendulum moved in a way that I guess was supposed to mean "No."

Hector shrugged. "It's weird," he said. "I'm getting nothing at this place tonight. Remember how active it was two years ago?"

"Yeah," I said. "It hasn't been that active here lately."

This wasn't exactly true; the last time I'd taken a student group there, the curtains had been moving and one kid got a photo that looked a lot like a woman's face standing just behind the window. Most shots like that turn out to be pictures of lamps, but still, it was pretty strange. However, Hull House hadn't seemed active even 10 percent of the times I'd been there in the last year.

The crystal pendulum thing struck me as a little bit silly—I always feel a little bit silly when I see people talking to rocks and expecting a response. But I remembered one of the reasons Hector and I made such a great team on the tours: some people *wanted* to be told that there was a portal to the netherworld over by the fountain or that a swinging crystal would tell us where the ghosts were if we addressed it politely enough. I wasn't about to do any of that, but Hector didn't have a problem with it. It ended up being the same skeptic/believer dynamic that Ken and I had when we did tours together.

And so we proceeded on to the place I really wanted to go to that night—Old Town (formerly Odin) Tatu. It was too far away from downtown to be a nightly stop on the tours, but Hector hadn't been in the building since that very first investigation, shortly before Tapeworm's death.

So we drove out there and got everyone to sign the waiver. (Since the basement wasn't set up for customers, we had to get people to sign a waiver saying they were going down those stairs at their own risk, in case they fell down, hit their head on the low ceiling, or saw a ghost and had a heart attack.) Then we headed inside.

I had gotten to a point where I could usually tell if it was going to be active in the basement as soon as I stepped inside, and that particular night, I really wasn't feeling it. Plenty of people were taking orb pictures, but those are always to be expected in places as dusty as that basement.

Hector looked around for a minute, soaking it all in, re-membering where the "Walter" voice was, where the cold spots had been. We walked around and sort of recreated that investigation. Hector broke out his pendulum, but had no luck with it.

Finally, he pulled out his camera and whispered, "Richie, brother. Tapeworm. Hombre." He then said something in Spanish and waited for a second, pointing his camera over at a dark corner, near where we'd heard the "Walter" voice.

Suddenly, he began to nudge me. "Look!" he said. "Something's moving over there."

I looked into the corner. Soon, everyone on the tour was looking over at that dark corner. Sure enough, it looked like *something* was moving over there, but it was too dark to see for sure.

We slowly approached, but by the time we got there, whatever had been moving was gone.

It wasn't until the next tour I ran with him a few weeks later that things got stranger. We were driving the bus down Division Street, through the area known around the city as the Viagra Triangle, due to the amount of middle-aged guys who roam through the bars on the strip trying to pick up twenty-year-old girls.

I joked about the strip as we stopped at a stoplight. Just as the light turned green, a big, bald dude with a goatee walked up and knocked on the door of the bus, smiling.

I smiled back and waved as we pulled away—people knocking on our doors or otherwise messing with us was nothing new, after all. It wasn't until we were pulling away that Hector and I both realized, at the same time, that the knocker looked awfully familiar.

"Dude!" I said. "Was that ... ?"

"Oh, my God!" said Hector. "You noticed it, too?"

I looked back at the picture of Tapeworm on the back of the bus. The knocker had looked *exactly* like him.

Traffic was pushing us forward, but I rushed to the back of the bus to look out of the rear windows. Naturally, there was no sign of any bald dude with a goatee.

Nothing out of the ordinary happened at the tattoo parlor that night. It appeared that the ghost of Tapeworm was out on the town.

Of course, hours later, I looked back on things and wasn't so sure. It probably wasn't Tapeworm's ghost—there were any number of bald dudes with goatees hanging around at the bars in the Viagra Triangle on any given night. After all, in addition to all of the bars geared at frat boys and old men on that strip, there's also a bar that features midget wrestling. You really do see all kinds on Division Street these days (instead of seeing nothing but low-down drunks and hookers, as you did a couple of generations back).

And the guy probably hadn't vanished as we drove away. He'd probably just stepped into a bar or something. Really quickly.

But, still. Maybe it was just our minds playing tricks on us. In fact, I should probably say it was *obviously* our minds playing tricks on us. But you know what? Maybe it wasn't.

It was a classic ghost encounter, the kind that most ghost stories spring from—a very brief encounter with someone or something that doesn't stick around long enough to answer any questions, leaving our imaginations to do the rest. Maybe that's all that ghosts are, really—the ability of our own minds to look at something as ordinary as a big weirdo knocking on the door of a tour bus and smiling or to feel "vibes" coming from something rattling in the furnace and turn it into something extraordinary.

Or maybe—just maybe—it really was some strange, otherworldly version of Tapeworm himself, out for a night of fun somewhere besides the musty basement of his old home, wanting to smile and say hello.

It was a few months later that I had perhaps the spookiest experience I've had yet. Right in the middle of a tour, too, which was a bonus.

The Congress Hotel had not been particularly active the whole time we'd been taking people there. The dark, empty ballrooms and corridors were spooky enough to make it a good enough place to stop even *without* a ghost showing up, but we hadn't had a lot of luck with pictures or actual sightings so far.

But in late summer of 2008, it started to seem creepier. That "haunted" vibe, which I'd never noticed there, started to be pretty distinctly present on tour stops there.

One particular night, as I stood in the lobby outside of the Gold Ballroom, I noticed blue, pink, and yellow lights dancing across the ceiling. The lobby was deserted, and the lights were mostly out. I didn't think I'd ever seen lights like that on the ceiling in there before, but figured that maybe I just hadn't noticed them. For the record, I didn't see them any other night thereafter, either.

Also, several people who wrote me after the tour said that they kept seeing shadowy forms out of the corner of their eyes while we stood there. I saw a couple myself, but brushed them off as tricks of the mind. There are mirrors all over the lobby, and they can pick up shadows of tourists and play tricks on you if you aren't really, really careful.

In the Gold Room itself, we had a weird battery-drainage issue—a couple of brand-new double As that had just been put into a camera suddenly went dead.

The spooky feeling followed us all the way up the stairs and down the hall to the Florentine Room. After telling the stories about it, I let the tourists in and began to lead them around, not bothering to turn on the light.

I was so spooked that night by the very feeling in the air that I decided, since it was dark and no one could see me looking foolish, to try out Hector's pendulum trick. I pulled out my key chain and let one of the attachments dangle.

"Key chain," I said politely, feeling only slightly dumb, "is there a ghost in here?"

The key chain swung a bit, seeming to point over at a wall where I had never heard of a ghost showing up. Satisfied that my makeshift pendulum had just been silly, I started walking back to the entrance, intending to turn the lights on. I was halfway back when the quiet of the room was broken by a very loud sound—like a gunshot—coming from the service hallway behind the wall where the key chain had been pointing.

A couple of people hit the deck. A couple of others asked if I'd set the whole thing up. A braver person ran into the hallway.

It was deserted. The whole floor, in fact, was deserted except for us. There had been no footsteps following the sound of the gunshot. There was nothing large on the floor that could have fallen to produce the sound.

We ended up spending the next several minutes trying to debunk the gunshot sound, but came up empty. If someone on the staff was playing a prank on us, they'd done a damned good job of it. Certainly, this was no "stuff a costume full of deer guts, stick it in the freezer and say it's Bigfoot" type of hoax. It was the kind that scared us so thoroughly that I almost had to make the next stop on the tour a trip to Target to buy new pants.

Two nights later, I was back in the Florentine Room, where a banquet had just been set up. Someone noticed a small 9-volt battery on the floor and dropped it to see if it made a noise similar to what we'd heard. It did, but it didn't explain the noise away. The night we'd heard the noise, we'd checked the vicinity *very* carefully, and we would've noticed a battery on the floor. Besides that, if a battery had just randomly fallen out of nowhere, that would be a paranormal event in and of itself.

Ken tried to tell me that the noise was probably just an oven closing or the furnace, two floors below, making noise. Just as Ken is known to think no one is psychic but him, he also tends not to believe in ghosts that other people report if he hasn't "sensed" them himself.

But a month or so later, Ken called me up in the middle of one of the tours he was running.

"We just heard the gunshot!" he said, proudly. "We checked the whole floor, and there's nothing here that could have caused it!" He gave up his idea that it was an oven or the furnace pretty quickly—the noise seemed far too close to be coming from the furnace, and there was no oven in operation anywhere near the floor.

This doesn't mean it was a gunshot, necessarily (by this point, the staff had taken to faking noises from time to time, though they usually owned up to it afterward), but this is the most we can truly hope for on a ghost hunt—we'd encountered something that simply defied explanation.

Being a ghost tour guide isn't *always* fun. As much as we mix up the tours, I do end up telling the same stories over and over. Sometimes I'm halfway through the story of the Iroquois Theater and realize that I've been thinking about cheeseburgers the whole time. Sometimes I just give up on ever actually seeing a ghost in a specific location. Sometimes the crowds are rowdy and unpleasant. The money isn't great—as a small operation, we could sell out every night and still not make much of a living out of it. Sometimes months go by without a single check coming in.

But then, every now and then, a moment like that comes along that makes everything old seem new again, and it's all worthwhile.

So You Wanna Hunt for Ghosts...

So, yes. I've seen some spooky stuff. I've investigated places where, in the heat of the investigation, I really did think there must be a ghost floating around. However, I'm no fool; I know perfectly well that there are always other explanations that can be offered and that we usually end up explaining even the best sightings away sooner or later. There's nothing I've seen that I truly expect to stand up to scientific investigation forever. But, on the other hand, who knows?

All I can say for sure is that we don't really *know* anything about ghosts. We have a few theories, but none that anyone can really agree on. All that this means, though, is that the questions are still open, and there's a lot left for us to find out. While I can't say that I expect anyone, anywhere, ever to find out anything for sure, I also sure can't discourage you from going out and looking for ghosts anyway. In fact, I heartily encourage it. It's fun and, often, a lot more educational than some skeptics might think. I may not have found a single actual ghost, but I've learned an awful lot about history and quite a bit about science that I wouldn't have otherwise learned. A lot about myself, too, as a matter of fact.

If you want to run a scientific ghost hunt of your own, it's really just as simple as gathering up some sober friends and saying, "Hey, gang, let's gather up our science gear and go look for ghosts!" After all, an investigation is really nothing more than sitting around an allegedly haunted place waiting for a ghost to show up. You can use practically anything you want for equipment, really.

Here in Chicago, we have a really terrific place called American Science & Surplus, which is like a RadioShack for mad scientists. They sell every manner of goofy scientific stuff, and they go out of their way to make it "fun." For instance, ball bearings are on sale under the name "robot eggs," and they are guaranteed to hatch within a million years or you get your money back (so keep your receipt). You can buy test tubes, Geiger counters, scales, weights, motors ... everything you need to built a shortwave radio, create a functioning robot, put together that hovercraft you've been dreaming of since third grade, or, just possibly, catch a ghost. In fact, I'd say that just about everything they sell there can be used in a ghost hunt, if you're willing to be a bit creative.

So, which stuff should you buy before you go on a ghost hunt? That's totally up to you, but you don't really *need* anything. It's nice to have some equipment, but frankly, there are only two real reasons to have any gear at all:

1. It can help give you clues as to where to look. Even if you get a weird reading on your equipment, it's not really "evidence," just a clue. You won't know if the reading really comes from a ghost unless an apparition shows up.

2. Gadgets are cool! How often do you get to use that EMF reader that's been gathering dust in your garage? If you spent seven grand to get yourself a thermal imaging camera for some reason, you might as well take it along on a ghost hunt. This is also the main reason so many ghost shows on TV use a ton of gadgets—flashing lights look neat on TV.

No one *really* knows what kind of gear you should use for a ghost investigation. We ghost hunters can argue about it all day. There's no piece of gear that will really determine whether a ghost is present, and it's to be assumed that the equipment that will react to a ghost being in the room will vary from ghost to ghost, since no two ghosts seem to be exactly alike. Some of them might be photographable only with one kind of camera, and others might only be visible in pictures taken by a totally different kind. Some ghosts might show up and bring a high radiation level with them. Others might show up and not change the radiation in the room at all. So who's to say which equipment to bring on the first trip to any given location?

But one thing we can pretty much agree on is that very little equipment on the market was designed for ghost hunting. The best way to figure out what gear is right for you is to experiment and customize.

No equipment is foolproof. Digital cameras may eliminate some of the problems ghost hunters had years ago with film cameras (like double exposure, scratches on the negative, and things like that), but they bring up new problems of their own. There are always, *always* other explanations for weird pictures. There are other explanations for *any* weird readings that any piece of gear turns up, in fact.

Ken and I generally feel that we don't need too much gear, since we have Ken and his superpowers. Like any other piece of equipment, he isn't foolproof, but he does the same thing that any other piece of gear would: he tells us where to look. Every now and then, he'll save us a lot of time by saying that he doesn't think any ghosts are present, which usually ends the investigation right away—if the psychic thinks a place isn't haunted, there's no way the group skeptic is going to want to stick around for any longer than it takes to look for secret passages, old tunnels, and the other non-ghostly stuff that you sometimes run into on investigations.

But if you don't have a reliable psychic to tell you where to look, there's plenty of gear on the market to play around with.

In fact, most people have all the equipment they need for a pretty good investigation stashed around the house. Different ghost hunters have different preferences as far as equipment goes—I think we can generally agree that you should use decent electronics as opposed to cheap, low-end stuff—but since we don't really know what ghosts *are*, exactly, we don't know what kind of equipment is really best. Every kind of gear has advantages and disadvantages. I once had someone tell me that with gear, or anything else, you have to pick two out of these three attributes: fast, cheap, and good. You can get something good and cheap, but it won't be fast. Or you can get something good and fast, but it won't be cheap, and something fast and cheap won't be good. And it's hard to imagine that something that isn't fast and good will be that useful in detecting ghosts.

Here are some of the standard gizmos:

1. Regular old tools

The tool we use the most is probably a level. People say that their doors are opening on their own, we show up and see that the doors are hanging crooked, and we're pretty much done. We might have to come up with *something* weird to tell them anyway. Some people would be absolutely devastated if we told them flat out that their house wasn't haunted, and I'm not in the business of making people feel stupid because they mistook something normal for something ghostly. But the vast majority of ghost reports *can* be explained away very easily. Screwdrivers and wrenches can tighten loose connections that cause weird noises and help you break into secret passages on occasion. You probably also have a thermometer lying around—these are good for checking out cold spots if you can't afford a thermal imaging camera (and you probably can't).

Some report that even the cheapest compasses will spin around wildly in your hand when a ghost is present—these can be good substitutes for more expensive electromagnetic field readers, and are much easier to use correctly. You can experiment with any tool in the world, really, though some are obviously more useful than others. For instance, I doubt you'll get much use out of a table saw on a ghost hunt. Try to use one, and you'll probably just end up getting hurt. Use your common sense (and safety goggles if you absolutely insist on using something dangerous).

2. Regular cameras

This is the most obvious one, really. You can't get a ghost picture without a camera. Now, what *kind* of camera you ought to use is a whole other matter. Every ghost-hunting group has their own theory about this one, and they can get pretty militant about it.

Digital cameras have been awfully controversial in the ghost-hunting community, and some ghost hunters get really uppity about using film instead. In 2003, Troy actually published an article called "Digital Cameras: Ghost Hunting at Its Worst." In those days, ghost hunters were seeing a barrage of low-quality digital pictures in which the orbs and mists were just the result of the digital camera reacting badly to low-light situations. It was argued that digital cameras were unreliable and that digital images were too easy to fake.

Things have changed a bit now. High-quality digital cameras are much easier to get now than they were in 2003. Even Troy no longer takes a hardline view against digital cameras (at least those that take pictures at 5 megapixels or more, which most of them do now). Some people still insist that film is automatically superior to digital; these are the same people who insist that tape recording is automatically preferable to digital audio (cough—nerds!).

The fact is that digital cameras and traditional cameras quite simply work in different ways. They react to and record light in different manners. Which method is really better for capturing ghosts frankly remains to be seen and may very well vary from ghost to ghost.

One thing that's worth noting, in fact, is that digital cameras pick up a broader range of light and colors than the human eye, and certain infrared lights that are invisible to the eye will be visible in digital cameras after they've been converted to that long series of 1s and 0s that make up a digital file. For instance, T-shirts have been made showing what appear to be clouds, but, when you take a digital picture, you'll be able to see lighting bolts emitting from the clouds in the picture. It may, in fact, turn out that the reason some ghosts are invisible is simply that they're composed of a kind of light outside the spectrum of human vision.

So, if you want to take some ghost shots, my advice is simply to find the best camera you can get your hands on. Use both film *and* digital, if possible. If you seem to be picking up a lot of orbs with a certain digital camera, try using another one—some cameras are simply prone to picking up false positives. Try it with and without the flash (though some people will tell you never, ever to use the flash on a ghost hunt).

With any kind of camera, you want to watch out for obvious things. Dust on the lens can create an "orb" shot. If the light from your flash bounces off something, that light can bounce back onto the lens, creating a perfectly round blob of light in the picture—an instant orb. Ghost hunters get pretty jaded to pictures of "vortexes"—vertical blobs of light that some people say are portals to another dimension, or something like that, but are usually just the camera strap. (Who knew that a three-dollar camera strap could be a portal to the netherworld?)

There's a similar argument over video cameras, of course. I practically never get anything good on video cameras, personally, and wading through the video looking for weird stuff is a lot more time-consuming than looking through photographs.

Also, I tend to think that video cameras are less likely to pick up a ghost. One reason we may not see a ghost with the naked eye could be that they only appear for a bare fragment of a second at a time, too quickly for the eye to see it. A camera taking a shot with a shutter speed of 1/1000th of a second per shot may pick up the ghost, if the shutter is opened at exactly the right moment, but the video camera (which is more likely to be taking shots at a speed of about 1/30th of a second) is less likely to pick up anything that your eyeballs wouldn't.

The way I explain this concept to people is to say, "Quick, how many fingers am I holding up?" I'll wave my hand in front of my face so quickly that no one can get a look at how many fingers are up with the naked eye, but if they'd take a picture of it with a fast shutter speed, they'd be able to see the fingers clearly. Perhaps ghosts just appear and disappear too fast—or move too quickly—for us to notice them.

So I suggest sticking with still cameras, for the most part, but if a ghost ever walks through a wall and starts chatting about the food in the afterlife on one of my tours, I know I'll wish I had a video camera on me.

Another thing to note is that some people are simply better at taking ghost pictures than others, it seems. Ken describes getting a picture of a ghost as being like getting a picture of lightning—you have to take the picture at exactly the right second, and some people just seem to have more of an instinct for it than other people. If you have some of these people in your group, have them use multiple cameras to make sure it's not just some quirk in their own cameras causing the "ghosts" to show up. When we have people taking a lot of strange pictures on the tour, we like to have them trade cameras with others and see if they still get more strange pictures than everyone else (which they do surprisingly often).

Other things to watch out for include smears and reflections in glass and "mist" that is actually breath hanging in the air on a cold day or smoke from a cigarette. Most investigations have a strict "no smoking" rule. The rules about drinking and joking get broken a lot, particularly in places where there doesn't seem to be anything ghostly going on, but the "no smoking" rule rarely does.

3. Infrared cameras

Some of the best ghost pictures of all time—or the coolest, anyway—were taken using infrared cameras.

Infrared light is a kind of light with a wavelength longer than the kind of light that is normally visible. In other words, it's light that exists all around you but that you can't see with your eyeballs. But infrared cameras and filters can convert infrared light into something you *can* see in the pictures. In addition to exposing "ghosts" that aren't visible to the naked eye, infrared filters are often used for, say, night vision goggles, which can be useful when poking around dark old buildings and graveyards for the simple reason that they'll help keep you from tripping over something in the dark and falling on your ass. In some circumstances, I understand that infrared goggles can even allow you to see right through people's clothes, if they're wearing the right kind of clothes and the right kind of underwear. Infrared stuff is getting cheaper; as a matter of fact, just about all digital cameras are actually infrared cameras by nature, but include a filter to filter out most of the infrared light, since it can lead to blurry shots. You can make yourself a filter that will block out other lights and get you infrared pictures, but to get decent shots using them you need a really long shutter speed (about a second in daylight, or ten seconds in dark areas), rendering them fairly useless for ghost hunts.

A much more advanced method of turning digital cameras into infrared cameras is to take your camera apart, locate and remove the infrared filter, then install a cobalt blue filter to block out everything *except* infrared light. The pictures taken with cameras like this are terribly cool, but the process of taking a camera apart and putting it back together is awfully tricky. I tried it and ended up with a broken camera, a pretty painful electric shock, and a wife with every reason to say, "I told you so." If you really want to give it a try, there are instructions all over the web, but be careful. Trust me.

4. Thermal imaging cameras

Occasionally ghost hunters get pretty cool images with these things, which are really just higher-tech color versions of infrared cameras (regular, "short" infrared shots are in monochrome). What they do is pick up colorful "heat signatures" that look sort of psychedelic. They can be pretty useful—if you're hearing a strange noise coming from somewhere in the attic, they can help you see if there's a rat or some other kind of critter up there making the noise. They're also a lot of fun—using stuff like this makes you feel like you're in a James Bond movie or something, and seeing what kind of heat signature you can pick up around toilets is always good for a laugh.

However, they cost a fortune. The only ghost hunters who normally use these things are groups who can talk a cable TV channel in bankrolling them. TV shows love these things, since they look so neat; it's useful to remember that even the most honest ghost-based TV programs have to do stuff that looks good on camera now and then.

The real use of thermal imaging cameras may not be finding ghosts so much as debunking them. Consider the night we heard the baby crying in the Garden of Evil. If we'd had a thermal imaging camera, we could have used it to see if there was a cat in the bushes or something. If we had one the night of the gunshot in the Congress Hotel, we could have seen if there were any footprints in the hallway. It wouldn't have necessarily solved the mystery for sure—I don't know how easy it is to tell a cat from a rabbit on these devices, and what we thought was a cat could have been, in reality, one of the garden's resident Bunnies of Evil, and it would be hard to tell *when* any footprints would have been left. But it would have given us quite a clue.

However, these cameras do sometimes pick up strange stuff. And there are a few very cool, entirely practical uses for them; for instance, if you're investigating a cemetery and the inscription on a tombstone has worn away, it might be legible when viewed with a thermal camera, since the place where the inscription *was* will have a slightly different heat signature than the rest of the stone. This is terribly cool to try.

And, of course, when you have a thermal imaging video camera, you will always, always know *exactly* who farted.

5. Audio recording gear

Audio recording gear has a similar debate to cameras—should you use tape or digital? Once again, tape recorders and digital recorders record sound in different ways, and anyone who claims that we can really know which of these methods is better for picking up ghostly voices is, not to put too fine a point on it, full of shit.

I use digital—it's simply easier for me. Tape recorders are bulky, noisy, and, generally, they record lower-quality sound than a good digital recorder. Also, you're going to want to put the audio file onto a computer—this is a lot easier to do with digital recorders. Generally, transferring tape to digital will result in even *more* loss of quality, unless you have some pretty expensive gear.

Of course, digital recording has its own problems. Digital voice recorders—anything that records in MP3 or another "lossy" format—will have some garbled sounds in the high frequencies. Artifacts from the process of compressing the sound and junk like that will lead to false positives. Most of the voice recorders on the market also have cruddy built-in microphones.

And microphones, too, are a question mark. It stands to reason that if you want to record the voice of a dead guy that is inaudible to normal hearing, you're probably going to want a pretty sensitive microphone. However, if your microphone is *too* sensitive, you can end up recording the voices of people outside or even in the building next door. You have to sort of strike a balance.

I use a small condenser microphone attached to a cheap attenuator—a little device with a knob on it that lets me turn the volume of the recording up or down, based on the environment. The mic is kept away from the recorder itself in an effort to avoid picking up the sound of the recorder.

I also prefer only to use recorders that allow me to listen to the recording as it's happening via headphones—being able to note times when I think I hear a weird noise right away saves a *lot* of time later.

6. An Internet connection

This, honestly, is probably the most important thing. You should find out everything you can about the history of the location that you're investigating. A lot of people have wasted a lot of time and cash looking for ghosts of people who never lived to begin with or aren't dead yet, and a bit of research could have saved them the trouble.

These days you'll probably be able to find more records online than you will at your local library. Several sites allow you to browse through online newspaper archives; census forms; war records; birth, marriage, and death records; and all kinds of neat stuff. Genealogy sites can be costly, but the good ones are worth it—I was able to download scans of my great-grandparents' (and Al Capone's) World War I draft registration forms, detailed records of my fourth great-grandfather's Civil War service, and other neat stuff—one site even showed me how I was an eighth cousin of Gerald Ford and an eighteenth great-grandson of Geoffrey Chaucer.

Census forms can show you whether a certain person, who is supposed to be haunting a house, ever existed in the first place, and if that person actually lived at the address in question. You can often use newspaper archives to determine the veracity of murder stories, train-wreck stories, and other such things, especially if the paper for the town in which you're conducting your investigation has an archive online—and more and more of them do. You can also frequently access old maps of cities online, and they can also come in handy—sometimes people will tell you, "Back then, when this haunted mansion was built, all of this area was just fields. There was only one dirt road for miles." They probably aren't *lying* to you, but they may be mistaken. Old maps can confirm or debunk the stories pretty quickly.

When we were putting together the Weird Chicago tour, Troy showed us an alley between State and Wabash that he had heard from a cop was the oldest street in Chicago. Maps showed that most of the major streets downtown were already in existence at a time when the street in question was still a beach on the shores of Lake Michigan (just about everything east of Dearborn Street was sand, in fact; the land was expanded several blocks farther east by a series of landfills over the years).

Digging up information is like a treasure hunt. When you find that news item from an Indiana newspaper—Indiana papers sometimes reported Chicago crimes that were left out of the Chicago papers—that shows that a hobo with a peg leg was actually murdered in a building where a peg-legged ghost has been reported, it's quite a rush.

In the past, you had to browse through archives on microfilm at the library for this sort of thing, which can be tedious and dizzying—I usually start to feel sick to my stomach after an hour or so on the microfiche machine, and I only use them now when I want to look up specific issues of defunct papers whose archives aren't online. Today, you can simply type an address into a newspaper archive online. But do your homework—addresses of buildings can change over the years. Chicago, for instance, renumbered most of the buildings in the city around 1909.

Another very important site, in my opinion, is www .snopes.com. This is a site that examines urban legends, old and new, and determines whether or not they have any basis in fact. One thing I can't emphasize enough is that the most important quality a ghost hunter can possess is the ability to call "bullshit" when necessary, not only in regards to ghost stories, but to historical stories and scientific claims. This site can be really, really helpful in developing that sort of mindset.

7. A bunch of goofy crap

Some ghost hunters like to use things like dowsing rods, crystals, and stuff like that. It probably can't hurt anything, as long as you remember to take what the stuff tells you with a grain or two of salt. And keep in mind that waving crystals around *will* make you look like a wacko to most people (sorry, Hector).

8. An electromagnetic field reader

You have one of these in your top dresser drawer, right? Doesn't everybody?

In recent years, these have been so common on ghost hunts that some people call them "ghost meters." Some are even marketed under the name "ghost meter," though showing up with such a thing on an investigation will usually have the same effect as just having someone write "novice" on your forehead. Remember, these things don't detect ghosts; they detect electromagnetic fields (EMF). Some people think that a jump in EMF means a ghost is in the room, but that may or may not really be the case.

EMF readers are used to measure energies in the room that are present all the time, but not visible. Most ghost hunters believe that ghosts are composed partly from electromagnetic energy, or that they use it to manifest, or something like that. No ghost-hunting kit is complete without some gear to measure energy in the room, and these are the most common.

Certainly places that are haunted tend to have a lot of strange stuff going on, electromagnetically speaking. But EMF readers can lead to false positives, just like anything else. If a reading is consistent along a straight line, it's probably an electrical wire causing the reading. They'll also give strong readings if you're anywhere near an appliance. Rooms where the EMF levels are high due to electrical gear in the room can actually create what some call a "fear cage," a room where high EMF levels can sort of play tricks on your brain and make you *think* there's a ghost around.

If you want to get one, there are a variety of options. The cheapest version is a Gauss meter, which can be purchased (as of this writing) for less than forty bucks. Better models go for hundreds.

One real problem is that practically nobody really knows how to use these things correctly. Very rarely do people using them on investigations actually calibrate them properly to begin with—most people just wave them around. Tilt your wrist just right, and you can make it look like the thing is going nuts. I've heard of tours that have people point them up at steeples of haunted churches, as if pointing it will somehow make it measure the EMF of an area two hundred feet in the air. Most EMF readers need to be set on the ground. You can only wave them around and get decent readings with the really expensive ones.

It's important to remember that a sudden, strange EMF reading doesn't necessarily mean that there's a ghost in the room—like all equipment, they can't tell you for sure if a ghost is around, they can just give you a good idea of where to look. Plenty of things besides ghosts can cause sudden jumps in EMF.

9. A Geiger counter

The use of Geiger counters in ghost investigations really took off in the 1970s. Like electromagnetic field readers, these are used to measure and detect energy—radiation, in this case—that isn't visible to the naked eye. Often, though not always, people who use them report that when a ghost shows up, there's a sudden drop in radioactivity in the room. Others say just the opposite: that ghosts cause a jump in radioactivity. Once again, a change in radiation doesn't mean a ghost is there—it's just a clue that you may be on the right track.

10. Motion detectors

Similar to thermal imaging cameras, these can be used for debunking ghosts more than they can be used to find them. You can use them to seal off a room and make sure that no one breaks in to mess with your stuff or to pull off a hoax on you. But they could also detect ghosts coming into the room, at least in theory.

Motion detection has been a part of ghost investigation since day one. If you don't have fancy electrical gear, you can "seal" a room the old-fashioned way: put some tape on the door, or have a piece of string running across the doorway. If the door is opened or someone walks through the doorway, the seal will be broken. Or, if the hoaxers aren't really careful, they'll trip on the string, fall on their faces, and everyone will have a jolly good laugh at their expense. You can call them hoaxers, and they can say, "I would have gotten away with it, too, if it weren't for you meddling kids!"

While I'm on the subject, in fact, all ghost hunters should be prepared for an awful lot of *Scooby-Doo* jokes. If you can't deal with this, or with people quoting *Ghostbusters* and asking where your proton pack is, you're going to have a rough time on investigations.

Troy's *Ghost Hunter's Guidebook* has an especially useful section on dealing with the media. When you get interviewed about ghosts for a local paper, he says, they probably aren't going to send the top reporter to talk to you; it'll usually be an intern who knows perfectly well that the easiest way to get an interesting article about you will be to make you look like a dork. And he guarantees you that the words "Who ya gonna call?" or "He ain't 'fraid of no ghost" will show up somewhere in the article. I'll vouch for that, too.

11. Séance gear

I'll tell you this right now: if you're a skeptic, it's gonna be *really* hard to sit around in a circle, holding hands with people and trying to get ghosts to knock on the table without feeling like a first-class ding-dong. But the old "sitting around a table, trying to get a ghost to ring a bell" routine is still going around, and if you go on a lot of investigations, people will ask you to do it sooner or later. Keep in mind how easy these things were to fake back in the days when they were all the rage. But also, keep in mind that a lot of people do report interesting results with this kind of stuff and that it probably can't hurt anything. One thing we certainly don't know about ghosts is how to get them to show up—maybe some ghosts just can't resist a table full of people holding hands.

Of course, by this logic, one could try any number of things to "attract them." Tapeworm said that he was sure that the ghosts were watching him have sex. I'm not aware of any groups who've used on-site orgies to attract spirits during ghost investigations, but if you're looking for an excuse to try, I just gave you one. You're welcome.

The biggest tool of the séances of old was a table. People would sit around it, usually holding hands, and try to get spirits to knock on the table. Groups of the same handful of people would meet regularly, and, as time went by, they would report the table vibrating, tipping, or producing knocking sounds, apparently of its own accord.

The weird thing about this is that if you're willing to sit with a group of people for a long enough time, it will almost always get results. The old-time spiritual people said that spirits were causing the vibrations of the table. Today, we usually say that it's little more than an example of the power of the human mind to create energies that will cause a notable physical impact on the environment, a sort of simplified version of the Philip Experiment. As such, you aren't likely to contact a ghost with this stuff, but what we can learn about the power of the mind from such experiments may eventually explain a lot about ghosts and how they come to be.

A somewhat more advanced—and usually faster—version of this is using a Ouija board. When people ask me about these, I usually tell them I don't think it's possible to talk to the dead using anything that says "Parker Brothers" on it. If you want to be really hardcore, many New Age shops will sell you homemade ones made of all-natural materials and other bells and whistles—one person even told me she had hers "blessed" by the person who sold it to her (I certainly hoped she tipped well for this). The problem with these things is that it's ridiculously easy for someone to fake it. Others say that the answers come not from ghosts, but from your subconscious, which seems reasonable. But this is precisely the reason a lot of people tell you *not* to use the boards—there are almost certainly things swimming around in your subconscious mind that you're not going to want to have bubbling to the surface.

I haven't actually used one myself since I was a teenager, when an old friend of mine and I used one to contact the spirit of an Illinois farmer and prankster who said his name was Gerard. He said he had a horse named Jorky, and I think a dog named Gev, and that he died in 1864 (I can't remember if it was the farmer or the horse who died that year). I'm not sure which of us was moving the thing—we probably both were—but I don't believe for a minute there was actually ever such a farmer. Then again, we got a pretty good story out of it, and you *do* hear a lot of stories about people using these things and contacting a person who *does* turn out to be a real person from history or something like that. Maybe these people are talking to spirits, maybe they're just demonstrating an interesting experiment digging into "collective subconscious" or something like that. I don't know.

One interesting side note is that back in 1920, the Baltimore Talking Board Company, which was making a version of the boards, tried to claim in court that they were spiritual tools, not toys, and, as such, should not be subject to taxation. They lost.

12. A good psychic

A lot of ghost hunters sneer at the idea of using psychics— and just about all skeptics do. This is because the vast majority of the people out there claiming to be psychics tend to turn out to be either nuts or just plain fakes. If you can find a down-to-earth, experienced psychic to come on an investigation, that psychic can work the same way any other piece of equipment does. You won't know for sure that a ghost is in the room because the psychic says so, but he or she can give you a clue as to where to look that's just about as reliable as a reading you'd get from an EMF reader.

The most important thing to have, honestly, is the right kind of mindset. You have to be skeptical enough to remember that there's going to be a scientific explanation for most anything that happens, but enough of an open mind to believe that there may be *something* in the room that can't be explained just yet. And remember rule number one: never charge money for your services. In the ghost-hunting community, people who charge for their services are looked upon like slimy, ambulance-chaser lawyers who go on TV and say, "Have you ever heard anyone sound as constipated as I do? Well, call me if you've been injured in an accident, and I can get you some great shit!"

Don't be that guy. Seriously.

And don't set fire to stuff. It's just common sense.

Proof?

In 1977, a woman named Teresita Basa was found dead in her Chicago apartment. Initially, it was thought to be a rape and murder case, but the autopsy revealed that there had been no rape—in fact, she was a virgin.

The police had no motive in mind, and no suspects, when a couple named Dr. and Mrs. Chua contacted the Evanston police and told them that Teresita had been "speaking" through Mrs. Chua, who worked at the same place as Teresita, though they didn't know each other. By speaking through her, Teresita had named her killer and said that the motive was her jewelry, which the killer had divided among his wife and various girlfriends.

The desperate police contacted the man fingered as the killer and found the jewelry just where "Teresita" told them it would be. The man confessed to the murder, then retracted the confession and entered a not guilty plea. Since the "voice from beyond the grave" wasn't the sort of evidence that would really hold up in court, the case seemed headed for certain mistrial when the killer, in a move that stunned the court, changed his plea to guilty against the advice of his attorneys.

Some people hold this case up as "proof" of the afterlife. Or "proof" of demonic possession. Or, at least, proof of ghosts.

Of course, it's none of those things. No one can *really* know if the Chuas were telling the truth or if they happened to have information from some other source and came up with the "voice from the grave" story as a cover for something. And, even if they were telling the truth, we don't have any idea as to the nature of what happened to make Mrs. Chua talk in Teresita's voice.

And that's the bottom line—we don't really know anything about ghosts.

People looking for "proof" of ghosts are going to be looking for a long, long time. Some people *claim* to have found it, but these people are pretty generally quacks. And if they prove that a ghost exists, the proof will only work for the one ghost they prove. It won't prove that any *other* ghost exists, necessarily.

Once, on a tour, I told people that we didn't think cemeteries were usually haunted.

"Well, then," said someone on the bus, "you don't know what you're talking about! My group has proven that they almost always are!"

They proceeded to show me a whole bunch of pictures of cemeteries. Orbs were all over in each of the pictures. These orbs, they said, were souls, trapped in purgatory, and their photos were proof of life after death.

I didn't call them idiots right to their face—that wouldn't have been polite. But a blurry picture full of balls of light isn't proof of anything. Even if I thought the orbs were something paranormal, not just dew points, fruit flies, dust or camera malfunctions, it wouldn't be proof of much. There was nothing in the picture to prove the existence of the soul, or of purgatory, or anything like that.

In dealing with the paranormal community, it's inevitable that you'll run across people or groups who will claim to have proven the existence of the paranormal, the supernatural, or the afterlife—they tend to have a glassy look in their eyes and tend to have trouble carrying on a conversation. Once I had a couple of people show me pictures of what they said were living dinosaurs. They held these up as proof of the biblical account of creation, and, therefore, the book of Revelations.

I don't know where to begin saying what was wrong with that. For one thing, the photograph was obviously a fake—the "dinosaur" was obviously computer-generated. Badly, for that matter. And even if it *was* a dinosaur, it would only be proof that some prehistoric species wasn't quite extinct yet, after all—something that's happened before, in fact; every now and then people *do* come across a living animal that was supposed to have gone extinct eons ago, such as the coelcanth, a fish that was thought to have died out with the dinosaurs, but was rediscovered in 1938. They might, in theory, be able to hold a living dinosaur up as *evidence* that the earth is only six thousand years old, not more than four billion, as scientists say, but it sure as heck isn't proof. Even if they proved that the earth was six thousand years old, it wouldn't prove that the creation story in the book of Genesis was the correct one, as opposed to one of the countless other creation stories in the world, and it sure as heck wouldn't prove anything in the subsequent books of the Bible.

It's the same way with ghosts, of course. Even if I took a picture of a transparent version of Tapeworm, and no one could find any way that I could have faked it, and it was very clearly Tapeworm, not just a dust particle or optical illusion, it wouldn't really *prove* anything. The fact is, there is no way to prove *anything* outside the field of pure mathematics. There's always another scientific explanation waiting around the corner, and there is always the chance that any piece of evidence could have been hoaxed. Everyone except for me would sort of have to take my word for it, and I'd have to take it as a matter of faith that no one had set me up with some sort of hologram technology or something.

Even with that possible Tapeworm sighting on Division Street under my belt and the gunshot in the Congress Hotel, I can't say with any certainty that I've ever seen or heard a ghost. And I don't really expect to.

Even people who live full-time in places that go down in history as haunted usually don't see things very often. The odds that we'll actually see something on a one-night investigation, or a fifteen-minute tour stop, are pretty slim—particularly if we don't happen to be there on an active night.

And even if I ever *do* have a girl disappear out of the bus as we drive through the old City Cemetery, what will it prove? That people come back from the dead? That mental energy can manifest as an apparition? That there's carbon monoxide on the bus?

The flip side of this is that ghosts are never going to be *dis*proven, either. There's never going to be a scientific discovery that makes ghost hunting completely pointless.

People pretty much believe what they want to believe. This is part of why phony mediums found it so easy to fool people during the height of the Spiritualist movement— people so desperately *wanted* to talk to their dead loved ones that they couldn't bring themselves to believe that that ectoplasm was just cheesecloth that had been stuffed up someone's butt. They believed it was their dead child because they desperately *wanted* to believe it.

I've seen this in action—if there's one question I dread more than "Do you believe in ghosts?" it's questions from people who want to contact a dead loved one or who believe that their dead child is haunting their house and want my help to prove it. If I were less honest, there would be a fortune to be made here. As I've said, I don't look New Agey. I don't claim that I can contact the dead or detect their presence. I look so young that I tend to get carded when I try to get into R-rated movies. Therefore, I probably come across as reasonably trustworthy and level-headed. But I've had people *beg* me to come to their house and confirm that their son is haunting it. I don't have to do a single thing to make them think I could do such a thing; they convince themselves. And many, I'm sure, would be prepared to offer me pretty impressive sums of money to confirm their beliefs.

I've yet to hear of a single séance in which the medium doesn't tell the client what he or she wants to hear. Consider that TV show where the woman claims to be contacting the spirits of people's dead pets—she never says anything like "Boy, did that cat hate you! I know she purred a lot, but she was totally faking it." The reasons for this are simple—if she tells the people what they want to hear, they'll want to believe her. If she tells them anything else, they'll start calling her a fraud. It happens a lot. If I tell people that the orbs they've photographed in the alley are just dust, some of them tend to get really ticked off and decide that I must not know what I'm talking about.

I'm always at a loss as to what to tell the people who are trying to contact someone. If I tell them I don't believe that there's anything haunting their house or that the pictures they have are just dust particles, they'd be devastated. At the same time, I have to stand on my principles and not lead them on just to make a quick, dishonest buck. About the best I can do is tell them that "I can't possibly confirm something like that, but if you think he's there, I'm in no position to say he's not."

How much of belief in ghosts comes from this sort of thing? How many of us decide that we believe in ghosts because someone we know claims to have seen one, and it's against our nature to think that our friends are kooks?

I'm no closer to answers than I ever was. Until that woman in white comes floating out of a wall to tell me to avenge her death and then submits to an interview, I won't be.

But that's part of why ghost stories endure. There are no answers. There never really will be. It's part of why they become such important parts of a town or family's identity. They may not be exactly true, but that's beside the point. Plenty of the historical facts that are part of our national identity as Americans—Christopher Columbus discovering America, Washington and the cherry tree, etc.—are no more reliable than the story of Resurrection Mary. But we know for sure that George Washington never cut down his father's cherry tree. We can keep on wondering about Mary.

As long as the city of Chicago stands, I imagine that I'll keep getting e-mails from restauranteurs saying that they

Troy, Adam, and Ken

think their restaurant is haunted. Some of them will be managers out to launch publicity stunts (we get a lot of those). Some of them will just be making up stories to explain noises that are really caused by bad wiring or rats in the basement. But other times, we won't be able to dig up an explanation for the hauntings, but we *will* find evidence of a murder or suicide in the building. And that'll start me on another long trail of research and detective work, and maybe give us a new place to stop on the tours. The supply of stories in this city is endless.

Weird Chicago Tours is doing well. We've expanded to run straight historical tours that barely mention ghosts, if at all, and several other spin-off tours that give me *more* reasons to do research into Chicago history. We've got a lot of plans for new tours, new stops, and new ways to get people around the city. And they'll keep expanding, because the stories just keep coming.

The ghost tours we run change all the time—we have an ever-growing list of places we can go, and sometimes months go by in which I never run the same route twice. The *Weird Chicago* book came out in summer of 2008, and immediately gave us a major boost. Hector and Willie are still driving for us. The tours still aren't a big moneymaker or anything, but business has picked up steadily; the *Weird Chicago* book has been especially good for business.

Ken and I are still doing investigations; lately we've been focusing on a couple of major sites around the city that we've been given unprecedented access to. Our reputation for having our heads more-or-less on our shoulders opens a lot of doors for us. I can't talk about many of them yet. Loose lips sink ships.

As of this writing, Olga and Ray are still in business, with a couple of new guides and drivers. The new guides seem friendly when we run into them. I ran into Olga herself at the St. Valentine's Day Massacre site (which we usually just drive by now, since there's not much to see), and we chatted pleasantly for a bit. Some stories are still going around (usually coming from Ray) that Ken and I were "fired" from Chicago Spooks or that Troy had lured us away with promises of more money, but, well, I suppose I've already covered that.

Ghost stories will stick around as long as people are still telling stories, as long as they're wondering what happens when we die, as long as we wonder how to explain the strange things that exist in the environment. There's no end in sight to any of that.

And, inevitably, as more stories are created, either by actual events or by sheer imagination, there will be more evidence—pictures, recordings, sightings that back up the ghost stories. They won't convert the unbelievers, but they'll reinforce the myths.

They won't be good evidence of ghosts.

But they will certainly be cool.

To Write to the Author

If you wish to contact the author or would like more information about this book, please write to the author in care of Llewellyn Worldwide and we will forward your request. Both the author and publisher appreciate hearing from you and learning of your enjoyment of this book and how it has helped you. Llewellyn Worldwide cannot guarantee that every letter written to the author can be answered, but all will be forwarded. Please write to:

Adam Selzer
℅ Llewellyn Worldwide
2143 Wooddale Drive. 978-0-7387-1557-5
Woodbury, Minnesota 55125-2989, U.S.A.

Please enclose a self-addressed stamped envelope for reply, or $1.00 to cover costs. If outside U.S.A., enclose international postal reply coupon.

 LLEWELLYN ORDERING INFORMATION

Order Online:
Visit our website at www.llewellyn.com, select your books, and order them on our secure server.

Order by Phone:
- Call toll-free within the U.S. at 1-877-NEW-WRLD (1-877-639-9753). Call toll-free within Canada at 1-866-NEW-WRLD (1-866-639-9753)
- We accept VISA, MasterCard, and American Express

Order by Mail:
Send the full price of your order (MN residents add 6.875% sales tax) in U.S. funds, plus postage & handling to:

> **Llewellyn Worldwide**
> **2143 Wooddale Drive, Dept. 978-0-7387-1557-5**
> **Woodbury, MN 55125-2989**

Postage & Handling:

Standard (U.S., Mexico, & Canada). If your order is:
$24.99 and under, add $4.00
$25.00 and over, FREE STANDARD SHIPPING

AK, HI, PR: $16.00 for one book plus $2.00 for each additional book.

International Orders (airmail only):
$16.00 for one book plus $3.00 for each additional book

Orders are processed within 2 business days.
Please allow for normal shipping time. Postage and handling rates subject to change.

Ghosts, Apparitions and Poltergeists

An Exploration of the Supernatural through History

BRIAN RIGHI

The perfect manual for the ghost enthusiast, aspiring ghost hunter, or anyone who likes spine-tingling true tales, this book has something for everyone! It looks at the stories behind famous ghosts through history, ghost hunting and the original ghostbusters, mediums, spirit communication, spirits, apparitions, poltergeists, and more. This ghoulish guide is unique because it blends the history of the paranormal and paranormal investigations (including some infamous cases) with the ghost stories that accompany them. It can be read as either a handbook for ghost hunters or a collection of true scary tales for pure enjoyment.

From ancient Babylon to nineteenth-century séance chambers to modern-day ghost hunts, paranormal investigator Brian Righi takes readers on a fascinating exploration of the supernatural. Readers will venture into creepy moonlit cemeteries, ghost ships, and haunted castles, learn how to conduct a ghost hunt of their own, and spend time with some of the greatest ghost hunters to ever walk through a haunted house.

978-0-7387-1363-2, 240 pp., 5³⁄₁₆ x 8 $15.95

The Case for Ghosts

An Objective Look at the Paranormal

J. Allan Danelek

What are ghosts? Can anyone become one? How do they interact with time and space? Stripping away the sensationalism and fraud linked to this contentious topic, J. Allan Danelek presents a well-researched study of a phenomenon that has fascinated mankind for centuries.

Analyzing theories that support and debunk these supernatural events, Danelek objectively explores hauntings, the ghost psyche, spirit communication, and spirit guides. He also investigates spirit photography, EVP, ghost-hunting tools, ouija boards, and the darker side of the ghost equation—malevolent spirits and demon possession. Whether you're a ghost enthusiast or a skeptic, *The Case for Ghosts* promises amazing insights into the spirit realm.

978-0-7387-0865-2, 240 pp., 6 x 9 $12.95

Haunting Experiences

Encounters with the Otherworldly

Michelle Belanger

Working the graveyard shift at a haunted hotel, encountering a Voodoo spirit in New Orleans, helping the victim of an astral vampire attack … the supernatural has played a part in Michelle Belanger's life since the age of three. Yet she refuses to take the "unexplained" for granted, especially when the dead speak to her.

From haunted violins to dark fey, Belanger relives her thrilling experiences with haunted people, places, and things. Inspired to understand the shadowy truths about these paranormal mysteries, she examines each otherworldly encounter with a skeptical eye. What remains is a solid survey of the paranormal from a credible narrator, who also learns to accept her own gifts for spirit communication.

978-0-7387-1437-0, 264 pp., 6 x 9 $15.95

How to be a Ghost Hunter

Richard Southall

So you want to investigate a haunting? This book is full of practical advice used in the author's own ghost-hunting practice. Find out whether you're dealing with a ghost, spirit, or an entity ... and discover the one time when you should stop what you're doing and call in an exorcist. Learn the four-phase procedure for conducting an effective investigation, how to capture paranormal phenomena on film, record disembodied sounds and voices on tape, assemble an affordable ghost-hunting kit, and form your own paranormal group.

For anyone with time but little money to spend on equipment, this book will help you maintain a healthy sense of skepticism and thoroughness while you search for authentic evidence of the paranormal.

978-0-7387-0312-1, 168 pp., 5³⁄₁₆ x 8   **$12.95**

Spanish edition:
Espíritus y fantasmas: Cómo investigar evidencias paranomales

978-0-7387-0382-4, 168 pp., 5³⁄₁₆ x 8   **$12.95**

True Hauntings

Spirits with a Purpose

HAZEL M. DENNING, PH.D.

How do ghosts feel and think? Do they suffer? Does death automatically promote them to a paradise, or as some believe, a hell? In *True Hauntings*, psychic researcher Dr. Hazel M. Denning recounts the real-life case histories of the earthbound spirits—both benevolent and malevolent—she has investigated. She also explores spirit possession, psychic attack, mediumship, and spirit guides.

978-1-56718-218-7, 240 pp., 6 x 9 $14.95

Ghost Worlds

A Guide to Poltergeists, Portals, Ecto-Mist & Spirit Behavior

Melba Goodwyn

From communicating with spirits to witnessing orbs burst from an inter-dimensional portal, Melba Goodwyn has seen it all as a psychic spirit investigator. In this fascinating examination of paranormal phenomena, she offers original insights into the nature of ghosts and haunting, true stories of her thrilling adventures, and practical ghost-hunting tips.

How are traditional ghosts different from poltergeists? How does a place or an object become haunted? What are orbs, ecto-mist, vortexes, and energy anomalies? Goodwyn defines different kinds of ghosts and entities, how they manifest, and why they are attracted to certain places.

978-0-7387-1195-9, 264 pp., 5³⁄₁₆ x 8 $14.95